30 Days Whole Foods Cookbook: Delicious, Simple and Quick Whole Food Recipes

Lose Weight, Gain Energy and Revitalize Yourself In 30 Days!

Disclaimer

Like all good foodies, we both know that there's no room for compromise when it comes to eating mouth-watering, delicious food that lights up your taste buds, sets your heart on fire and leaves your belly feeling satisfied.

That's especially true when it comes to those times in your life when you want to lose weight, boost your energy and feel incredible again.

And that's why I know you'll LOVE this cookbook.

It's more than just a collection of the most nourishing and scrumptious recipes. It will become your bible that will help switch the way you look at food, change the way you feel about yourself and realize that you can have your (healthy) cake and eat it. You can still eat your favorite foods and still lose weight.

However, please remember that I'm not a medical professional. I'm not a chef and I'm certainly not a doctor either. So please consult a medical professional before you make changes to your diet or lifestyle.

By eating the delicious food in this cookbook, you do so at your own risk and assume all associated risk involved. Not that there's anything to worry about, but it's worth mentioning anyway.

No responsibility is taken for any loss or damage related directly or indirectly to the information in this book. Never disregard professional medical advice or delay in seeking it because of something you have read in this book or in any linked materials.

Table of Contents

Introduction

The Standard Western Diet (the ultra-processed, high sugar, high processed fat, high additive and preservative kind) is making us all fat and sick.

It's leaving us malnourished, depressed, low in energy and struggling to make it through the day.

No matter our actual clothing size, we find ourselves feeling puffy and bloated, looking ten years older and wishing we could do something about the way we look and feel.

When we're feeling low, we dream about recapturing the energy we used to have as kids, shifting enough weight so we finally feel good enough to fit into that wedding dress or fasten the top button on our pants without having to suck our guts in.

We just want to feel good about ourselves.

The story normally goes that we find ourselves on Amazon, scrolling through the latest books on new diets and recipe books filled with 'weight loss recipes', trying to find a solution that might help.

Or perhaps you sign up for your local slimming club and follow their recommendations to eat low fat foods, ditch the carbs or swap your real meals for replacements.

Yet nothing works.

But here's the thing. Nothing works because it's not real. It's not real food and it's not a real solution.

All these things are temporary measures that help satisfy the urge inside of you to stand up and do something drastic. But they don't work long term.

You still find yourself reaching for food in moments of crisis because that's what you've always done.

You still punish yourself with food, treat yourself with food.

You still love food, but you hate it with all your heart and soul.

Your relationship with food stays the same as it always has been and so nothing ever changes.

A better solution that works

The problem here is that we can't fix a lifetime of unhealthy eating patterns by putting a Band Aid over the top.

The same wound will still be there. You won't heal.

When you stop the diet, when you rip off the Band-Aid, you'll still see the same gaping wound and you'll repeat the same patterns.

So, if you want to make lasting change to your life, if you want to transform the way you look and feel, we need to take a different approach.

That is when the wholefoods approach comes in.

It's not a fad diet. It's not a Band-Aid. It's not a quick fix that will only last a month before you go back to your old eating habits. It's real.

Instead of eating those crappy processed foods which are largely nutrient devoid and leave you feeling 'yuck', you'll be eating foods which are packed full of everything your body needs to thrive.

You'll nourish yourself from the inside, you'll feel satisfied, your hair and skin and nails will start glowing with health and you'll feel incredible.

You won't have to count calories, consider grams of fat or limit your portions at all because your body will naturally help you regulate what you eat.

Sound good? Yeah, I thought I would. That's why I wrote this book- to help you get the same amazing results as I did when I quit eating crap and started to take care of my body.

Although I wanted to write a pure recipe book that would focus on the wholefood diet, I also wanted to help others discover this wonderful lifestyle. This means I've briefly included information on what the wholefoods diets are all about, what you can and can't eat and a few tips on how to get started.

Once we understand these easy guidelines, we'll dive straight into the recipes and I share with you a range of meals including satisfying breakfasts, mouth-watering lunches, inspiring dinners, tasty treats and snack and even sauces and dips. I've tried to provide as much value as I can for you so I've included a range of recipes that can be made on your stove and in your oven, as well as in your crockpot and in your Instant Pot. Wherever possible, I've made sure most of these recipes are as quick as possible to make. However, there are times where I've gone ahead and included a recipe for you anyway, simply because it's so delicious.

So, without further ado, let's get welcome in the changes and help you feel as healthy, happy and slim as you deserve.

Chapter 1: What is the Wholefoods Approach?

Before we get into the recipes, let's take a few moments to understand a few of the guidelines relating to the wholefood diet and lifestyle. Don't panic- there's nothing crazy difficult on the list here.

It's all common sense.

What can you eat?

The rules are simple. Eat real food.

This means you can eat as much meat, seafood and eggs as your heart desires. You can pile your plate with delicious fresh, juicy fruits and vegetables, include natural fats, spice up your life with herbs, spices and other seasonings.

You can eat whatever you like, provided that it's as close to its natural state as possible and contains just a handful of ingredients (that you recognize and can pronounce!!)

Sounds awesome, right?

What can't you eat?

Now at this stage, I'd prefer to keep it perfectly simple and utterly positive. But I know that I also need to make sure that when you're feeling hungry and you're finding yourself miles from home and completely unprepared, you know exactly what you can put into your body.

Here's a better breakdown of what you need to avoid for the next 30 days:

1. **Sugar.** Avoid eating any kind of sugar whether that is real or artificial. This includes natural sweeteners such as coconut sugar, stevia, date syrup, xylitol, honey, monk fruit extract and maple syrup.
2. **Alcohol**. Alcohol is also a potent source of sugar and is bad for your body so avoid it for these 30 days.
3. **Grains**. Grains such as wheat, rye, barley, oats, corn, rice, millet quinoa and buckwheat are off the menu, as are derivatives such as wheat bran, wheatgerm, puffed rice and so on.
4. **Legumes.** Bad news for vegetarians- beans and lentils are off the menu. This includes black beans, chickpeas, kidney beans, fava beans and even peanuts (including peanut butter).

5. **Dairy.** Say no to all types of milk, cheese, cream, ice cream, frozen yoghurt and other non-plant-based dairy.
6. **Baked goods and junk foods.** The whole foods diet is about avoiding processed foods, so you'll also need to avoid baked goods like pancakes, cakes, cupcakes, pasta, granola and so on, even if it says it's approved.
7. **Additives.** Additives like carrageenan, monosodium glutamate and sulfites are bad news for your body. Avoid.

What?? No meal plans for the wholefoods diet?

If you've ever looked online to find information about the wholefoods diet or Whole30, you're likely to have been faced with piles of confusing information, a seemingly endless number of meal plans and much more else besides that you need to wade your way through.

But I like to keep it simple. That's why, instead of sharing a detailed 30-day eating plan with you, I've decided to do things differently.

I understand if you're rolling your eyes at this point and asking yourself why you bothered buying this book. I don't blame you. But hear me out.

You see, I have a much better idea up my sleeve that I know you will love- the fully customizable diet blueprint that will take you from where you are today through the next 30 days and well beyond.

It will also help you to be creative, design something unique that fits your tastes and lifestyle and have some fun whilst you're doing it.

Here's how it works.

1) You grab yourself a sheet of paper and write a grid with the days of the week down on side and the meals along the top. Include space for snacks too if you want.
2) Check out the delicious recipes in this book and then pencil them into your meal plan, along with the page number. You can do this by working through all breakfasts, all lunches, all dinners, all snacks, and so on, or you can simply work your way through the book and see what takes your fancy. It's up to you.
3) Use these recipes to make yourself a grocery list then grab your reusable bags and head to the grocery store. If you're feeling overwhelmed at this point, just buy enough for the next 2-3 days.
4) Come home, store as much as you can in the fridge to keep fresh and then get cooking! *Easy!*

Other guidelines and rules you should know...

There are a few other rules that you should bear in mind when starting a wholefood diet. They include:

1) Don't weigh or measure yourself more than once over the 30 days.
2) Don't take daily photos to track your body shape changing
3) Don't obsess over your weight, how your clothes fit or whether you still have that stomach.
4) If you choose to follow this lifestyle after the first 30 days, feel free to add back in legumes and grains. (If you don't have any food sensitivities).

The wholefoods plan is about so much more than how you look and thinking about it will just waste energy that would be better spent doing fun things and enjoying how incredible you will feel.

Ready for the recipes? Awesome! Let's get to it.

Chapter 2: RECIPES

Breakfast

Sweet Potato and Caramelized Onion Breakfast Casserole

When you wrap your lips about this incredible breakfast dish, you'll hardly believe that it's actually good for you. If you're not a fan of spouts, switch for another green leafy veg.

Serves: 10
Time: 1 hour 15 mins

- Calories: 254
- Net carbs: 8g
- Protein: 12g
- Fat: 18g

Ingredients:

- 12 slices sugar-free bacon, cut into 1" pieces
- 2 large sweet potatoes, peeled and sliced into thin rounds
- 2 tablespoons melted coconut oil
- Sea salt, to taste
- 3 cups Brussels sprouts, tops removed and chopped
- 1 large onion, sliced
- 12 free-range eggs
- 1/3 cup coconut milk
- 1/4 cup nutritional yeast
- 1/2 teaspoon garlic powder
- Black pepper, to taste

Method:

1. Preheat your oven to 425°F, grease a 9 x 13" casserole dish and line a baking sheet with paper.
2. Place a skillet over a medium heat and add the bacon, cooking until crisp. Remove from the skillet and pop to one side.
3. Meanwhile, place the sweet potatoes into a casserole dish, toss with cooking oil, sprinkle with salt and pop to one side.
4. Place the Brussel sprouts onto the baking sheet and do the same as you did for the potatoes.
5. Pop both trays into the oven and cook for 20-30 minutes until soft. Once cooked, remove from the oven.
6. Place the onion into the skillet and cook for five minutes until soft.

7. Add a pinch of salt and stir again, then continue cooking the onions on a very low heat for 20 minutes until soft and dark.
8. Grab a bowl and add the eggs, coconut milk, yeast, salt, pepper and garlic powder. Stir well to combine.
9. Turn the oven down to 400°F then grab the casserole dish.
10. Add the Brussel sprouts to the dish followed by the onions, bacon and egg mixture.
11. Bake for 25 minutes until firm then remove from the oven.
12. Serve and enjoy!

Sweet Coconut Cauliflower Rice

This sweet coconut rice makes a perfect breakfast on those days you just want some comfort food. Fast and delicious, you can also add homemade applesauce, sliced bananas or the toppings of your choice to make it better than ever.

Serves: 2-4

Time: 20 mins

- Calories: 173
- Net carbs: 2g
- Protein: 17g
- Fat: 2g

Ingredients:

- 1 head cauliflower, riced (about 5 cups)
- 1 tablespoons coconut oil
- 1 teaspoon cinnamon
- ½ teaspoon nutmeg
- Coconut milk, to taste

To serve...

- Homemade applesauce
- Bananas
- Raisins
- Nuts and seeds

Method:

1. Place a skillet over a medium heat and add the coconut oil.
2. Add the cauliflower, spices and coconut milk if using, stir well and cook for 10 minutes until soft.
3. Serve and enjoy with the toppings of your choice.

Spinach Artichoke Breakfast Casserole

Loaded with veggies and packed full of healthy wholefood protein, this spinach and artichoke casserole is a dish you'll find yourself making time and time again. It stores brilliantly, so feel free to make a batch and then store it for later in the week.

Serves: 10

Time: 50 mins

- Calories: 235
- Net carbs: 3g
- Protein: 11g
- Fat: 18g

Ingredients:

- 8-10 slices sugar-free bacon
- 2 medium sweet potatoes, peeled and sliced into thin rounds
- 1 medium onion, chopped
- 3-4 cloves garlic, finely chopped
- Sea salt, to taste
- 10 oz. fresh baby spinach, chopped
- 14 oz. can artichoke hearts, drained and chopped
- 12 large free-range eggs
- 1/2 cup coconut milk
- 3 tablespoons nutritional yeast (opt)
- 1/2 teaspoon sea salt
- 1/4 teaspoon black pepper
- 1/4 teaspoon onion powder (opt)

Method:

1. Preheat the oven to 400°F and grease a 9 x 13" casserole dish with oil.
2. Grab a bowl and add the sweet potato, oil and salt then place into the casserole dish.
3. Pop into the oven and cook for 30 minus until soft. Remove from the oven.
4. Place a skillet over a medium heat and add the bacon, cook until crispy then pop to one side. Retain 1 tablespoon of cooking fat.
5. Turn the heat down then cook the onions for five minutes. Add the garlic and cook for a further minute.
6. Throw in the spinach and salt, leave for a minute to wilt then add the artichoke hearts.
7. Stir everything through then remove from the heat.

8. Grab a large bowl and add the eggs, coconut milk, salt, pepper, onion powder and nutritional yeast and whisk well.
9. Spoon the artichoke mixture over the sweet potato, pour the egg mixture over the top then pop into the oven.
10. Cook for 25 mins until the top starts to brown.
11. Remove from the oven and leave to sit for 10 minutes.
12. Serve and enjoy.

Sweet Potato Apple Breakfast Bake

There are times when you just need a hit of sweetness (and coffee!!) to get you going in the morning. If this sounds like you then make yourself this incredible breakfast bake. Rich in antioxidants, healthy proteins and just the right combo of crunch and taste, it's a keeper, that's for sure

Serves: 4-6
Time: 30 mins
- Calories: 127
- Net carbs: 10g
- Protein: 24g
- Fat: 3g

Ingredients:
- 1 large sweet potato, peeled and shredded
- 1 large pink lady apple, peeled and shredded
- 2 tablespoons coconut oil
- 1/8-1/4 teaspoon fine grain sea salt
- 1 teaspoon cinnamon
- 1/4 teaspoon nutmeg
- 2 free-range eggs, whisked
- 1/2 cup coconut milk
- 1/4 cup raisins (opt.)
- Chopped pecans (opt.)

Method:
1. Preheat your oven to 400°F then pop some coconut oil into a skillet and place over a medium heat.
2. Add the sweet potatoes to the skillet and cook until they start to get soft.
3. Add the apples, salt and spices and cook for a further five minutes.
4. Grab a medium bowl and add the eggs and the coconut milk. Whisk well until combined then pour over the potatoes and apple.
5. Sprinkle with raisins and pecans then pop into the oven for 10 minutes until the eggs are set and slightly brown.
6. Remove from the oven, leave to rest for a minute or two then serve and enjoy!

Sweet Potato Breakfast Hash

Call me crazy, but sometimes I need a spicy hit in the morning. Do you feel me? That's when I turn to this mouth-watering breakfast hash. It's a great dish to kick-start your day and you can have a ton of fun switching up the ingredients in the spice mix.

Serves: 5

Time: 25 mins

- Calories: 382
- Net carbs: 19g
- Protein: 18g
- Fat: 25g

Ingredients:

- 2 medium sweet potatoes, peeled and diced small
- 1 lb. ground pork, chicken or beef
- Salt and pepper, to taste
- 1 large honey crisp apple, diced
- 3 cups kale, chopped
- 1-2 tablespoons water or broth
- 2-3 tablespoons ghee or coconut oil, divided

For the spice mixture...

- 1 teaspoon cinnamon
- 1/2 teaspoon onion powder
- 1/2 teaspoon garlic powder
- 1/2 teaspoon sage
- 1/2 teaspoon turmeric

Method:

1. Grab a skillet, add a tablespoon of coconut oil or ghee and place over a medium heat.
2. Add the meat, sprinkle with salt, pepper and half the seasoning. Stir well, cook until brown and then set aside.
3. Find another skillet and add the remaining ghee or coconut oil.
4. Throw in the potatoes, season with more salt and pepper and cook for 5 minutes.
5. Cover the skillet with the lid and cook for another five minutes until soft.
6. Remove the lid and add the apples, late and water.
7. Cover again then cook for another minute or two.
8. Uncover and sprinkle with the seasoning.
9. Add the meat to the potato mixture, stir well then serve and enjoy.

Mexican Breakfast Casserole

Spicy and filling, with just the right amount of kick, this Mexican-inspired dish makes the perfect weekend brunch and is packed with juicy peppers, succulent sausages and just the right amount guilt-free cheesy flavor. Enjoy.

Serves: 8

Time: 1-hour 10mins

- Calories: 271
- Net carbs: 10g
- Protein: 20g
- Fat: 16g

Ingredients:

- 2 medium sweet potatoes, peeled and sliced into thin rounds
- Coconut oil, as needed
- Sea salt, to taste
- 1 medium onion, diced
- 1 large or 2 small red bell peppers, diced
- Pinch of salt
- 1 lb. sausages (sugar free)
- 12 large free-range eggs
- 1/3 cup coconut milk
- 1/2 teaspoon salt
- 1 teaspoon chili powder
- 1/2 teaspoon cumin
- 1/4 cup nutritional yeast
- 1 cup sugar free salsa

To serve...

- Fresh cilantro
- Avocado

Method:

1. Preheat your oven to 425°F and grease a 9x 13" baking dish with coconut oil.
2. Place the sweet potato into the bottom of the dish, sprinkle with salt and roast for 30 minutes.
3. Meanwhile, grab a skillet, add a tablespoon of olive oil or ghee and place over a medium heat.
4. Add the onions and pepper and cook for five minutes.
5. Add the sausage and cook for a further few minutes, stirring well

6. When the sweet potato is cooked, remove from the oven, pop to one side and lower the heat to 400°F.
7. Grab a large bowl and add the eggs, coconut milk, nutritional yeast, chili powder, cumin and salt. Whisk well.
8. Place the sausage over the sweet potatoes, spread the salsa over the top then pour the egg over everything.
9. Pop into the oven for 30 minutes until set.
10. Remove from the oven, leave to rest for a few minutes then serve and enjoy.

Sweet Potato Ground Turkey Scramble

Turkey makes a satisfying and nourishing breakfast scramble that works perfectly with cardamom and cinnamon for your wholefood breakfast. Throw in some apple (not in this recipe but an awesome extra) and you'll have an incredible meal that will please the whole family.

Serves: 6
Time: 45 mins

- Calories: 261
- Net carbs: 4g
- Protein: 21g
- Fat: 13g

Ingredients:

- 1 lb. ground turkey
- Coconut oil or ghee, to taste
- 1 leek, sliced thinly
- 1/2 teaspoon cardamom
- 1/4 teaspoon cinnamon
- 1/4 teaspoon salt
- 2 sweet potatoes
- 7 large eggs
- 7-10 mushrooms

To serve...

- Green onions

Method:

1. Preheat the oven to 350°F.
2. Grab a skillet, add a small amount of cooking oil then place over a medium heat.
3. Add the turkey and the leeks and cook until the turkey is browned. Drain off any excess grease.
4. Add the cardamom, cinnamon and salt, stir well then pop to one side.
5. Make slits into the sweet potatoes then pop into the microwave to cook for 7-8 minutes until soft.
6. Remove from the microwave and slice open, then leave to cool
7. Grab a medium bowl, add the eggs and whisk well.
8. Find your mason jars then add a spoonful of sweet potato, 3 tablespoons of the turkey and ¼ cup of the egg mixture to each.
9. Top with 4 sliced mushrooms then another scoop of sweet potatoes.
10. Pop into the oven for 20-25 minutes then leave to cool for a few minutes.
11. Serve and enjoy.

Sausage Pizza Egg Muffins

These snack-sized muffins make a fantastic grab-and-go breakfast, snack or something more substantial when you need more traditional fueling. Packed with Italian flavor, they'll make your mouth water and your taste buds go crazy

Serves: 12

Time: 35 mins

- Calories: 142
- Net carbs: 4g
- Protein: 9g
- Fat: 9g

Ingredients:

- 3/4 lb. sugar free pork sausage
- 2 cloves garlic, minced
- Dash crushed red pepper
- 2/3 cup chopped sun dried tomatoes
- 2 teaspoons Italian seasoning blend
- 1 teaspoon onion powder
- 9 free-range eggs
- 1/4 teaspoon fine grain sea salt
- 1-2 teaspoons coconut oil

Method:

1. Preheat the oven to 400°F and grease 12 cup muffin tin with coconut oil or olive oil.
2. Grab a skillet, add 1-2 teaspoons coconut oil and place over a medium heat.
3. Add the sausage and red pepper and cook until nearly brown.
4. Add the sundried tomatoes and cook for a minute then remove from heat and set to one side.
5. Grab a large bowl and add the eggs, onion powder, Italian seasoning and salt. Whisk well to combine.
6. Scoop the sausage mixture into the eggs and stir well to mix.
7. Spread the mixture between the muffin cuts and pop into the oven.
8. Bake for 15 minutes until set and just beginning to brown.
9. Leave to cool for a few minutes then serve and enjoy.

Soup & Stews

Stuffed Pepper Soup

Super easy, super-fast and super delicious, this soup is sure to claim its place on your 'go to' list and keep your stomach fueled no matter what you throw at it.

Serves: 8

Time: 25 mins

- Calories: 221
- Net carbs: 8g
- Protein: 16g
- Fat: 12g

Ingredients:

- 1 lb. ground beef
- 1 tablespoons ghee
- 1 medium onion chopped
- 5 cloves garlic, minced
- Sea salt, to taste
- 1 1/2 teaspoons sugar-free Italian Seasoning
- 1 teaspoon paprika
- 3 bell peppers, chopped
- 3 cups bone broth
- 15 oz. can tomato sauce
- 3/4 teaspoons fine grain sea salt

For the cauliflower rice...

- 2 cups cauliflower "rice"
- 1 tablespoons ghee
- 1/4 teaspoon onion powder
- 1/4 teaspoon garlic powder

To serve...

- Minced parsley

Method:

1. Grab a large pan, add the ghee and pop over a medium heat.
2. Add the ground beef and cook until browned, stirring frequently.
3. When the beef is almost browned, add the onions and garlic and cook for another 3-5 minutes.
4. Throw in the salt, Italian seasoning and paprika and cook for 30 seconds or so.
5. Add the peppers, broth, tomato sauce and salt and stir through.

6. Over with the lid then bring to the boil.
7. Turn down the heat to a simmer and cook for 5-10 minutes until all the ingredients are cooked through.
8. Make the cauliflower rice and stir through the ghee, onion powder and garlic powder.
9. Serve together and enjoy.

Instant Pot Chicken Rice Soup

This chicken soup is a great dish to make on the weekends and keep serving all week long. Although it's simple, fast and pretty effortless for any day of the week. Packed with veggies and flavor, it will keep you warm and nourished, no matter what the weather is doing outside.

Serves: 6
Time: 30 mins

- Calories: 258
- Net carbs: 7g
- Protein: 25g
- Fat: 14g

Ingredients:

- 2 tablespoons ghee
- 1 medium onion, diced
- 4 cloves garlic, minced
- 8 oz. mushrooms, sliced
- 1 cup carrots, cut into bite size pieces
- Sea salt and pepper, to taste
- 1 lb. boneless skinless chicken breasts
- 2 teaspoons poultry seasoning, dried
- 4 cups chicken bone broth
- 1/2 cup coconut cream (opt)
- 2 teaspoons tapioca flour
- 1/2 tablespoons brown mustard (opt.)
- Sea salt and pepper, to taste
- 8 oz. cauliflower rice

To serve...

- Chopped parsley or chives

Method:

1. Open the lid of your Instant Pot, add the ghee and turn onto sauté mode.
2. Add the onions, mushrooms, carrots and garlic. Cook for five minutes until becoming soft.
3. Take the chicken, season well then place into the pot.
4. Pour the broth and seasoning over the pot then cover with the lid.
5. Cook on manual high for 10 minutes.
6. Do a quick pressure release then remove the chicken.
7. Transfer to a plate and shred with two forks. Pop to one side.

8. Turn the Instant Pot onto sauté mode then add the tapioca flour, coconut cream and mustard.
9. Stir gently as the sauce thickens.
10. Add the chicken and the cauliflower rice to the pot and cook for another minute.
11. Turn off then serve and enjoy.

Cold Cucumber & Avocado Blender Soup

When it's hot outside and you just want something fast, create this effortless soup. Packed with refreshing cucumber and avocado, it's light, tasty and awesome.

Serves: 2

Time: 10 mins

- Calories: 180
- Net carbs: 23g
- Protein: 9g
- Fat: 20g

Ingredients:

- 1 avocado, chopped
- 2 cups cucumbers, chopped
- 1/4 cup cilantro leaves
- 1/2 teaspoon salt
- 1/2 jalapeno, seeded
- 1 tablespoon lime juice
- Zest of half of a lime
- 1 clove garlic, chopped

Method:

1. Grab a high-speed blender, throw in all the ingredients and hit that whizz button.
2. Blend until smooth.
3. Serve and enjoy.

Roasted Butternut Squash Soup

Ever tried roasted butternut squash? If not, you're in for an absolute treat. Creamy, sweet an incredible, it will warm you from the tips of your toes to the top of your head.

Serves: 4
Time: 1 hour

- Calories: 373
- Net carbs: 45g
- Protein: 6g
- Fat: 19g

Ingredients:

- 4 1/2 lb. whole butternut squash, sliced in half lengthways and seeds removed
- 3 tablespoons ghee, melted and divided
- 4 cups chicken stock
- 1/2 cup coconut milk
- Salt, to taste

To serve...

- Fresh thyme leaves
- Extra virgin olive oil

Method:

1. Preheat your oven to 425°F and lightly grease a baking tray with ghee or coconut oil.
2. Place the butternut squash onto a chopping board, cut in half lengthwise then scoop out the seeds.
3. Place onto the baking tray (cut side down) then cook for 45 mins to an hour until cooked.
4. Remove from the oven and place the butternut squash into a high-speed blender.
5. Add a cup of the stock and blend until combined.
6. Add extra stock, one cup at a time until your soup is at just the right consistency.
7. Add the coconut oil and season with salt. Whizz again.
8. Serve and enjoy.

Bacon Cauliflower Soup

This creamy cauliflower soup reminds me of the cauliflower cheese dishes my mother used to make for the family when we were kids. If you want to add a cheesy tang, add liberal sprinklings of nutritional yeast. Omit the bacon and switch the broth for a veggie version if you like.

Serves: 6
Time: 30 mins

- Calories: 130
- Net carbs: 7g
- Protein: 9g
- Fat: 7g

Ingredients:

- 4 slices thick-cut bacon, chopped
- 1 onion, chopped
- 2 carrots, chopped
- 1 celery stick, chopped
- 1 teaspoon coconut oil
- 3 garlic cloves, minced
- 3 cups chicken broth
- 1 x 14 oz. can coconut milk
- 1 head cauliflower, chopped into florets
- 1 teaspoon sea salt, or more to taste
- ½ teaspoons ground black pepper

To serve...

- Chopped parsley

Method:

1. Place a large pot over a medium heat then add the bacon.
2. Cook for 5 minutes until crispy then pop to one side.
3. Place the onion, carrots and celery into the pot, stir well and cook for five minutes.
4. Remove the veggies from the pot and pop to one side.
5. Pour the coconut milk into the pan and add the garlic and stir well. Cook for a minute or so.
6. Add the broth, coconut milk and cauliflower and bring to a boil.
7. Turn down the heat and simmer for 10 minutes until the cauliflower is cooked.
8. Remove from the heat then use an immersion blender to puree until smooth.
9. Add the onion, carrot and celery back to the pan, season with salt and pepper and simmer for five more minutes.
10. Remove from the heat, sprinkle with bacon bits and parsley then serve and enjoy.

Mushroom, Kale and Chicken Soup

This soup is just what the doctor ordered when its feeling cold outside. Cook the chicken ahead of time to create soup that is fast, tasty and will please a crowd.

Serves: 4

Time: 25 mins

- Calories: 343
- Net carbs: 14g
- Protein: 27g
- Fat: 19g

Ingredients:

- 1 lb. cooked chicken thighs, skin and bones removed
- 3 tablespoons ghee
- 2 leeks, chopped
- 3 cloves garlic, minced
- 2 cups white button mushrooms, sliced
- 2-3 large handfuls kale, roughly chopped
- 2 tablespoons + 2 teaspoons arrowroot starch or tapioca
- 2 2/3 cups chicken bone broth
- 2/3 cup coconut milk
- 2 tablespoons nutritional yeast
- 1/2 tablespoons brown mustard
- 2 sage leaves, minced
- 2 teaspoons fresh minced rosemary
- Sea salt and pepper, to taste

Method:

1. Grab a large pan, add the ghee or coconut oil and pop over a medium heat.
2. Add the leeks, mushrooms and garlic and cook until soft.
3. Add the kale and stir through.
4. Take a small bowl, add the arrowroot and add a small amount of broth, stirring until smooth.
5. Add the rest of the broth to the arrowroot and stir through.
6. Pour the arrowroot and coconut milk into the veggies and stir through.
7. Add the mustard and nutritional yeast then stir until combined.
8. Bring to a boil then simmer on low.
9. Add the chicken, herbs and seasoning.
10. Heat through then serve and enjoy.

Salads

Harvest Chicken Salad with Herbed Aioli

Easy to throw together and perfect with the aioli, you'll probably find yourself making this packed-lunch perfect salad again and again. Yum!

Serves: 6

Time: 15 mins

- Calories: 291
- Net carbs: 8g
- Protein: 16g
- Fat: 20g

Ingredients:

For the herbed aioli...

- 2/3 cup mayonnaise (see recipe here)
- 1 teaspoon fresh rosemary, minced
- 1/2 teaspoon fresh sage, minced
- 1/2 teaspoon thyme, minced
- 2 cloves garlic, minced
- 1/4 teaspoon onion powder
- 1/2 teaspoon lemon juice

For the salad...

- 1 lb. chicken breast, cooked and chopped
- 1 medium apple, diced
- 1/3 cup Brussels sprouts, chopped or shredded
- 1/4 cup dried cranberries, no added sugar
- Sea salt and pepper, to taste

Method:

1. Grab a medium bowl, add the ingredients for the aioli and stir well. Pop to one side.
2. Find a large bowl, add the salad ingredients then stir well.
3. Add the mayonnaise, season with salt and pepper and stir again.
4. Serve and enjoy.

Asian Chicken Chopped Salad

Add an Asian twist to your chicken salad by using this brilliant recipe. Free from soy and sugar, it will fill you up and keep you satisfied all day long.

Serves: 8
Time: 15 mins

- Calories: 139
- Net carbs: 8g
- Protein: 5g
- Fat: 7g

Ingredients:

For the salad...

- 4 cups coleslaw mix
- 1 cup shredded red cabbage
- 1/2 red bell pepper, sliced thin
- 1 cup shredded chicken breast
- 1/4 cup slivered almonds
- 2 green onions, finely sliced
- 1 tablespoon sesame seeds (opt.)

For the dressing...

- 1/4 cup coconut aminos
- 2 tablespoons rice vinegar
- 2 tablespoons extra virgin olive oil
- 1/2 tablespoon sesame oil
- 1 teaspoon minced garlic
- 1 teaspoon grated fresh ginger
- 3 large pitted dates

Method:

1. Grab a large bowl, add the salad ingredients and toss to combine.
2. Take a blender, add the dressing ingredients then whizz until smooth.
3. Pour the dressing over the salad and toss to combine.
4. Serve and enjoy.

Harvest Chicken Salad

IMHO, this chicken salad is a cut above the rest. Featuring delicious roasted sweet potatoes, rosemary, avocado, raspberries, pomegranate and even nuts, it ticks just about every nutritional box and leaves you feeling amazing.

Serves: 4
Time: 25 mins

- Calories: 281
- Net carbs: 30g
- Protein: 10g
- Fat: 15g

Ingredients:

- 4 chicken thighs boneless, skinless
- 1 tablespoon rosemary fresh, minced
- 1 tablespoon sage fresh, minced
- 1 teaspoon garlic powder
- 1 tablespoon olive oil
- Salt and pepper, to taste

For the sweet potatoes...

- 1 large sweet potato, cubed
- 2-3 tablespoons olive oil
- 1 tablespoon arrowroot flour
- 1 tablespoon rosemary fresh, minced
- 1 teaspoon salt
- 1/2 teaspoon red pepper flakes

For the dressing...

- 1/3 cup balsamic vinegar
- 1/4 cup olive oil
- 2 tablespoons date sauce
- 1 teaspoon stone ground brown mustard
- 1/4 teaspoon salt
- 1/4 teaspoon red pepper flakes, opt.

For the salad...

- 4-6 cups spring mix baby greens
- 4-6 cups baby arugula
- 1 cup fresh raspberries
- 1 cup pomegranate seeds

- 1/2 cup walnuts, raw or toasted
- 1/4 cup pumpkin seeds, raw or toasted

Method:

1. Preheat your oven to 425°F then grease a baking tray.
2. Grab a skillet, add some olive oil and pop over a medium heat.
3. Find a bowl, add the chicken, spices and olive oil and then toss until completely coated.
4. Place the chicken into the skillet and cook until crispy.
5. Remove from the pan and pop onto a plate to cool slightly. Slice into strips once cool.
6. Grab another bowl and add the sweet potato, spices, olive oil and arrowroot flour. Stir well to combine.
7. Place onto the baking tray and bake for 30 minutes until golden.
8. Find a small bowl, add the dressing ingredients then stir well until combined.
9. Take your serving bowl or plate and add the greens, chicken, sweet potatoes, remaining salad topping and drizzle the dressing over the top.
10. Serve and enjoy.

Broccoli Cauliflower Salad

Who'd have thought that broccoli and cauliflower could taste so good? Certainly not me. Simple and fast, this recipe tastes brilliant. Up the protein content by throwing in chicken or whatever other meat of your choice. If you're veggie, tofu also works great.

Serves: 6

Time: 10 mins

- Calories: 269
- Net carbs: 7g
- Protein: 6g
- Fat: 22g

Ingredients:

- 2 1/2 cups broccoli, chopped into florets
- 2 1/2 cups cauliflower, chopped into florets
- 1 cup red bell pepper
- 1/3 cup bacon bits

For the dressing...

- 1/2 cup mayonnaise (recipe available in this book)
- 2 tablespoons olive oil
- 1 tablespoons lemon juice, chopped into small florets
- 1 tablespoon fresh thyme
- 1/2 teaspoon garlic powder
- 1/2 teaspoon sea salt
- 1/4 teaspoon black pepper

Method:

- Find a large bowl and combine the broccoli, cauliflower, red pepper and bacon bits.
- Take a small bowl and add the dressing ingredients then stir well to combine.
- Pour the dressing over the salad then stir well to combine.
- Serve and enjoy.

Steak Salad Steakhouse-Style

Steak salad? Tomatoes? Cucumber? Ranch dressing? Eggs? Olives? Avocados? Yes, your mouth is probably watering right now, and quite rightly. Enjoy.

Serves: 4

Time: 15 mins

- Calories: 308
- Net carbs: 10g
- Protein: 18g
- Fat: 20g

Ingredients:

For the steak...

- 12 oz. sirloin steak
- Sugar-free Cajun seasoning, to taste
- 2 tablespoons ghee

For the salad...

- 1 small head romaine lettuce, washed and sliced into about 1 1/2" slices
- 1 Roma tomato, diced
- 1/3 cucumber, diced
- 8 free-range eggs, soft- or hard-boiled
- 1/4 cup kalamata olives
- 2 ripe avocados, peeled and sliced
- Homemade range dressing, to taste (recipe available in this book)

Method:

1. Place the steak onto a large plate and season well with the Cajun seasoning.
2. Grab a skillet, add some ghee then place over a medium heat.
3. Cook the steaks for around 2 minutes on each side then remove from the pan. (Cook longer if you like your steak well-done.
4. Leave to rest for five minutes.
5. Grab a large bowl and add the salad ingredients. Toss well to combine.
6. Place the steak over the top of the salad then drizzle with the ranch dressing.
7. Serve and enjoy.

Kale Salad with Crispy Sweet Potato

Healthy, low carb and stunningly tasty, this salad balances texture and taste perfectly to create an epic lunch that you're sure to make time and time again.

Serves: 4
Time: 35 mins
- Calories: 300
- Net carbs: 19g
- Protein: 10g
- Fat: 10g

Ingredients:
- 6 cups chopped kale, stems removed
- 1 tablespoon olive oil
- 1 tablespoon vinegar
- 3 free range eggs, hardboiled and cut into quarters
- 4 strips sugar-free bacon, fried and chopped
- ½ avocado, chopped

For the sweet potatoes...
- 2 large sweet potato, peeled and cut into fried shape
- 1 tablespoon olive oil
- Pinch of salt and pepper, to taste
- 1 teaspoon paprika
- 1 teaspoon garlic powder

Method:
1. Preheat your oven to 450°f and grease a baking sheet with a small amount of olive oil.
2. Grab a large bowl and add the sweet potato, olive oil, salt, pepper, paprika and garlic powder. Stir well to combine.
3. Place the potato onto the baking sheet and pop into the oven for 10 minutes.
4. Turn then cook for another 10 minutes until crispy.
5. Meanwhile, take a large bowl and add the kale, olive oil and vinegar.
6. Massage the kale for 2-3 minutes until it starts to soften.
7. Add the eggs, avocado and bacon and stir gently.
8. Serve with the sweet potato fries and enjoy.

Strawberry Spinach Salad

Yes, strawberries in a salad. Not convinced? Then try this and try telling me you're not a convert! With spinach, basil, avocado and nuts, it's the perfectly balanced meal in a bowl.

Serves: 4
Time: 15 mins
- Calories: 319
- Net carbs: 7g
- Protein: 13g
- Fat: 26g

Ingredients:

For the dressing...
- 1/4 cup coconut milk or coconut cream
- 1/4 cup avocado or olive oil
- 2 tablespoons apple cider vinegar
- 3 tablespoons lemon juice
- 2 teaspoons dried mustard
- 1 1/2 teaspoons poppy seeds
- Salt and black pepper, to taste

For the salad...
- 4 cups baby spinach
- 1 tablespoon fresh basil or mint, finely chopped
- 1 1/2 cups sliced strawberries
- 1 avocado, diced
- 1/3 cup chopped pecans or walnuts plus extra for topping
- 1 cup shredded cooked chicken, leave out for meatless version
- 2 tablespoons slivered almonds

To serve...
- Green onions, to taste

Method:
1. Find a medium bowl and add the ingredients for the dressing. Stir well then pop to one side.
2. Take a large bowl and add the salad ingredients. Pour the dressing over the top and toss to combine.
3. Sprinkle with additional chopped pecans then serve and enjoy.

Mango Cilantro Curry Chicken Salad

This Asian-inspired salad asks you to cook the chicken from scratch, but you really don't have to if you want to slash time from the cooking process. Use cooked chicken and you can enjoy this surprising salad faster.

Serves: 6
Time: 35 mins

- Calories: 469
- Net carbs: 19g
- Protein: 28g
- Fat: 32g

Ingredients:

For the chicken...

- 1.5 lb. chicken breast
- Salt and pepper, to taste

For the dressing...

- 1 cup mayonnaise (recipe available in this book)
- 2 tablespoons curry powder
- 2 tablespoons white wine vinegar
- 2 tablespoons fresh lime juice
- 2 teaspoons Dijon mustard
- 1 mango, skinned, seeded, and diced
- 3 tablespoons fresh chopped cilantro plus more to serve
- Pinch salt

For the salad...

- 3/4 cup chopped celery
- 1/4 cup diced green onion
- 1/3 cup sliced almonds
- 1/4 cup raisins

Method:

1. Preheat your oven to 350°F and grease a baking tray.
2. Place the chicken breast onto a flat dish, season well then pop into the oven for 25 minutes until cooked through.
3. Remove from the oven and leave to rest for ten minutes.
4. Cut into small pieces or shred with two forks.
5. Meanwhile, find your blender and add the ingredients for the dressing. Whizz until smooth.
6. Take a large bowl and add the chicken, salad ingredients and dressing.
7. Stir well then pop into the fridge until ready to serve.
8. Serve and enjoy.

Kale Chicken Caesar Salad

Caesar salad has always been one of my favorite salads of all time, and this one certainly doesn't disappoint! Creamy, succulent and delicious, it's one of my favorite go-to salads ever.

Serves: 5

Time: 15 mins

- Calories: 422
- Net carbs: 9g
- Protein: 11g
- Fat: 39g

Ingredients:

For the dressing...

- 1/2 cup mayonnaise (recipe available in this book)
- 2 teaspoons fresh lemon juice
- 2 teaspoons coconut aminos
- 2 cloves garlic, minced
- 2 teaspoons spicy brown mustard
- 1/8-1/4 teaspoon sea salt, or to taste
- 1/8-1/4 teaspoon black pepper, or to taste

For the salad...

- 5 cups kale, chopped
- 1 1/2 tablespoons olive oil
- 3/4 cup pine nuts
- 1 teaspoon olive oil or coconut oil
- 1 boneless skinless chicken breast
- Sea salt and black pepper, to taste
- 1/2 large avocado or 1 small, diced

Method:

1. Grab a small bowl and add the dressing ingredients. Stir well to combine then pop to one side.
2. Place a skillet over a medium heat and add a small amount of oil.
3. Season the chicken with salt and pepper then place into the skillet. Cook for 6-7 minutes on each side until cooked through.
4. Pop to one side, covering with foil to keep warm.
5. Place a small skillet over the heat, add a small amount of oil then add the pine nuts. Sprinkle with salt then cook for a minute or so until brown.
6. Grab a large bowl and add the kale and 1 ½ tablespoons olive oil.

7. Sprinkle with salt then massage for a few minutes until it becomes softer.
8. Add the avocado and pine nuts and toss.
9. Remove the chicken from the foil and slice before laying on the top of the salad.
10. Drizzle with the dressing then serve and enjoy.

Avocado Caprese Salad

This vegetarian salad is effortless to make and makes a wonderful main meal when you're pushed for time, or a brilliant side salad when you need something fresh and packed with nutrients. Yum!

Serves: 6

Time: 10 mins

- Calories: 197
- Net carbs: 12g
- Protein: 2g
- Fat: 17g

Ingredients:

- 4 medium heirloom tomatoes, sliced into rounds
- 3 medium avocados, sliced
- 1 large bunch fresh basil
- Juice of 1 lemon
- 1 tablespoon organic extra virgin olive oil
- White wine vinegar, to taste
- Sea salt and fresh ground pepper, to taste

Method:

1. Place the tomato slices into a bowl and lightly salt.
2. Next pop the avocado into a smaller bowl, cover with the lemon and then toss carefully
3. Layer the tomatoes, avocado and basil, drizzle with vinegar and oil then serve and enjoy.

Lunch Ideas & Side Dishes

Butternut Squash Fries

Who needs potato fries when you can have these healthy, tender and amazing fries?

Serves: 4

Time: 50 mins

- Calories: 216
- Net carbs: 41g
- Protein: 2g
- Fat: 7g

Ingredients:

- 1 medium butternut squash, cubed
- 2 tablespoons ghee or coconut oil
- 1/2 teaspoon sea salt
- 1/4 teaspoon black pepper

Method:

1. Preheat your oven to 400°F and grease a baking sheet.
2. Place the butternut squash onto the baking sheet, drizzle with oil, season well then pop into the oven for 40 minutes.
3. Serve and enjoy.

Garlic Roasted Radishes

If you told me that roasted radishes were good, I would never have believed you. In fact, it wasn't until I went to a potluck in my neighborhood that I tried them for the first time. All I can say is...WOW!

Serves: 4

Time: 25

- Calories: 78
- Net carbs: 3g
- Protein: 1g
- Fat: 1g

Ingredients:

- 1 lb. radishes, ends trimmed and halved
- 1 tablespoon melted ghee or butter
- 1/2 teaspoon sea salt
- 1/4 teaspoon pepper
- 2–3 garlic cloves, finely minced
- 1/4 teaspoon dried parsley, dried chives or dried dill

Method:

1. Preheat your oven to 425°F and grease a baking sheet.
2. Grab a bowl and add the radishes, ghee, salt and pepper and stir until coated.
3. Place onto the baking sheet then pop into the oven for 20 minutes.
4. Remove from the oven, add the garlic and parsley and cook for a further five minutes until brown.
5. Serve and enjoy.

Green Beans with Crispy Bacon

Beans...bacon...you really can't go wrong, can you?

Serves: 4

Time: 10 mins

- Calories: 63
- Net carbs: 4g
- Protein: 2g
- Fat: 4g

Ingredients:

- 3/4 lb. green beans, trimmed
- 3 strips pastured bacon, diced
- 1/4 cup chopped basil
- 1/4 cup chopped parsley
- 1 clove garlic, crushed
- Salt, to taste
- 1 tablespoon olive oil or ghee

Method:

1. Place a pan of water over a medium heat, bring to the boil then drop in the steamer.
2. Add the beans then steam until cooked.
3. Meanwhile, place a skillet over a medium heat, add the bacon and cook until brown.
4. Remove from the heat and stir through the garlic.
5. Place the beans into a serving bowl, add the bacon then toss.
6. Serve and enjoy.

Brussels Sprouts Salad with Bacon & Apple Vinaigrette

You'll find that even the pickiest of kids (or adults) will love these Brussels sprouts. With apples, bacon, hazelnuts and a delicious vinaigrette, they're simply out of this world.

Serves: 10

Time: 25

- Calories: 292
- Net carbs: 13g
- Protein: 5g
- Fat: 24g

Ingredients:

For the dressing...

- 3 tablespoons apple juice
- 3 tablespoons apple cider vinegar or lemon juice
- 1 tablespoons mustard brown or Dijon mustard
- 1 1/2 tablespoons date paste
- 1/2 teaspoon cinnamon
- 1/2 teaspoon onion powder
- 1/2 cup light olive oil or avocado oil
- Sea salt and black pepper, to taste

For the salad...

- 1 lb. brussels sprouts raw, shredded, sliced very thinly
- 8 slices sugar-free bacon, cut into pieces
- 1 tablespoon rendered bacon fat
- 2/3 cup hazelnuts, chopped
- Sea salt, to taste
- 1 medium apple, chopped
- 2 teaspoons lemon juice
- 1/2 cup dried cranberries, sugar free

Method:

1. Place a skillet over a medium heat and add the bacon.
2. Cook until brown then remove and place onto a paper towel to drain. Retain the cooking fat.
3. Grab a large bowl, add the sprouts, the bacon and a tablespoon of the cooking fat then toss well.
4. Place the skillet back over the heat then add the nuts, sprinkle with salt and cook for five minutes.

5. Add the nuts, apples, lemon juice and cranberries to the sprout mixture then stir again.
6. Grab a small bowl and add the dressing ingredients. Stir well to combine then drizzle half over the salad. Keep the rest to add as required.
7. Serve and enjoy.

Mexican Cauliflower Fried Rice

This fried rice meal is amazingly filling and when topped with ranch dressing, guacamole, veggies and healthy protein, it will keep you satisfied through even the toughest of workout.

Serves: 6

Time: 30 mins

- Calories: 335
- Net carbs: 5g
- Protein: 15g
- Fat: 27g

Ingredients:

- 1 head cauliflower, riced (approx. 12 oz.)
- 1 lb. ground beef turkey, chicken, or pork
- 3 tablespoons olive oil or ghee, divided
- 1/2 teaspoon fine grain sea salt
- 1/2 teaspoon onion powder
- 1/2 teaspoon garlic powder
- 1 teaspoon cumin
- 1 teaspoon chili powder (opt.)
- 1 red bell pepper, diced
- 1 small yellow onion, diced
- 3 garlic cloves, minced
- 1 can chopped green chilis
- 1 jalapeno pepper, seeds removed and minced

To serve...

- Cilantro

For the guacamole...

- 1 large ripe avocado or 2 small, mashed
- 2-3 tablespoons onion, minced
- 1 clove garlic minced
- 1-2 tablespoons jalapeno peppers, minced
- 1 1/2 tablespoons fresh lime juice
- 2 tablespoons chopped fresh cilantro, plus more for garnish

Method:

1. Pop a skillet over a medium heat and add a tablespoon of coconut oil.
2. Add the meat to the skillet, sprinkle with salt and spices and cook until browned.
3. Add the onions and pepper, stir and cook for a minute or two.

48

4. Throw in the chilis, garlic and jalapeno and cook for another minute or two.
5. Place the cauliflower rice into the pan, stir well to coat then cover the skillet with the lid. Cook until the cauliflower is soft.
6. Remove the skillet from the heat and pop to one side.
7. Find a medium bowl and add the guacamole ingredients, and mash well.
8. Serve and enjoy

Scalloped Potatoes

These amazing potatoes do take time to cook, but it's largely hands-off so you can go and do something else whilst it's cooking in your oven. It's also perfect for meal prep as it stores well in the fridge for several days. Yum!

Serves: 3-4

Time: 1 hour 25 ins

- Calories: 587
- Net carbs: 94g
- Protein: 10g
- Fat: 21g

Ingredients:

- 3 lb. organic Russet potatoes, sliced thinly
- 1/4 cup ghee
- 1/4 cup cassava flour
- 1 1/2 cups water
- 1 cup unsweetened almond milk
- 1 tablespoon garlic oil
- 1 1/2 teaspoons salt
- 1 tablespoon fresh thyme
- 1 tablespoon fresh chopped rosemary
- 1/2 teaspoon pepper

Method:

1. Preheat your oven to 325°F and grease a 13 x 9" baking dish with ghee or coconut oil. Pop to one side.
2. Find a small saucepan and add the ghee and cassava flour. Stir well to combine and then turn on the heat.
3. Cook for around a minute then add the water, almond milk and garlic oil then whisk as it continues to cook. This should take around 5 minutes.
4. Add the salt, thyme, rosemary and pepper and stir well, then remove from the heat.
5. Pour a thin layer of the sauce into the baking dish then add a layer of potatoes.
6. Repeat with the remaining sauce and remaining potatoes until everything is used.
7. Cover with foil then pop into the oven for 45 minutes until browned and cooked through.
8. Serve and enjoy.

Garlic Parsnip Fries with Bacon Aioli

There's nothing like the taste of parsnip fries to wake up your taste buds and treat you to something different. Teamed with bacon aioli, it's a low carb, tangy and creamy side dish that will make any foodie proud.

Serves: 4
Time: 40 mins

- Calories: 322
- Net carbs: 14g
- Protein: 3g
- Fat: 26g

Ingredients:

- 3-4 medium parsnips, peeled and cut into 1/2" thick "fries"
- 1 1/2 tablespoons ghee or olive oil
- 3-4 cloves garlic, minced
- Salt and pepper, to taste
- 3 slices sugar-free bacon, cooked until crisp and crumbled
- 1/2 cup mayonnaise (see recipe here)
- 1 1/2 teaspoons fresh lemon juice
- 3 cloves garlic, minced
- 1/2 teaspoon spicy brown mustard
- Sea salt, to taste

To serve...

- Minced parsley

Method:

1. Preheat the oven to 425°F and grease a large baking sheet.
2. Grab a large bowl and add the parsnips and the melted ghee. Toss well to combine.
3. Spread the parsnips over the baking tray then pop into the oven.
4. Bake for 20 minutes until brown.
5. Remove from the oven then sprinkle with the garlic.
6. Pop back into the oven and bake for another 10 minutes.
7. Serve and enjoy.

Sweet & Savory Harvest Sweet Potato Hash

Perfect for the holidays or any time you need a hug from the inside, this hash combines veggies, nuts and even apples with warming spices. Delicious!

Serves: 2-4

Time: 40 mins

- Calories: 188
- Net carbs: 14g
- Protein: 2g
- Fat: 13g

Ingredients:

- 1/2 teaspoon ground sage
- 1/4 teaspoon dried thyme
- 1/4 teaspoon dried rosemary
- Pinch black pepper
- 1/2 teaspoon cinnamon
- 1/8 teaspoon allspice or ground cloves
- 1/8 teaspoon nutmeg
- 1/2 teaspoon onion powder
- 1 large sweet potato, diced into 1/2" cubes
- 12 oz. Brussels sprouts, cut in halves
- 1 1/2 tablespoons avocado oil
- 2 tablespoons + 2 teaspoons coconut oil, divided
- 2 medium apples, diced the same size as sweet potato
- 3/4 cup pecan halves
- 1/2 teaspoon sea salt (plus more as needed)
- 1/4 cup dried cranberries, unsweetened

Method:

1. Preheat the oven to 425°F and grease a baking sheet.
2. Take a small bowl and add the spice mixture ingredients. Stir well to combine.
3. Find a large bowl and add the brussels sprouts, the olive oil and a teaspoon of the spice mixture.
4. Pop into the oven and cook for 15 minutes.
5. Remove from the oven, add the pecans, stir well then pop back into the oven for another five minutes or so.
6. Meanwhile, place the remaining oil into a skillet, pop over a medium heat and add the sweet potatoes.
7. Sprinkle with the salt then cover with a lid.

8. Cook for a few minutes then uncover, stir and cover again. Cook until the potatoes are soft and light brown.
9. Add the apples and stir to combine then cook for a further five minutes.
10. Turn off the heat, add the remaining spice mixture, cranberries, sprouts and pecans then stir through.
11. Serve and enjoy.

Carrot Fries with Bacon and Rosemary

Just when you thought there wasn't any other way you could beat potato fries, along comes carrot fries with their scattering of rosemary and bacon and buckets of flavor.

Serves: 6

Time: 35 mins

- Calories: 176
- Net carbs: 9g
- Protein: 4g
- Fat: 12g

Ingredients:

- 2 lb. carrots, peeled and cut into 'fries'
- 1 1/2 tablespoons avocado oil or light olive oil
- 1/4 teaspoon sea salt
- 1/8 teaspoon black pepper
- 1/2 teaspoon onion powder, optional
- 2 tablespoons fresh rosemary, minced
- 6 slices sugar-free bacon

Method:

1. Preheat your oven to 425°F and grease a baking sheet with a small amount of oil.
2. Grab a large bowl and add the carrots, oil, salt, pepper, onion and rosemary. Stir well to combine.
3. Place the carrots onto a baking tray and pop into the oven.
4. Cook for 15 minutes then remove from the oven and flip.
5. Return to the oven and cook for another 10 minutes or so.
6. Remove from the oven again, sprinkle with the cooked bacon and pop back into the oven for a minute or two.
7. Remove from the oven and then serve and enjoy!

Bacon Garlic Spaghetti Squash

Although we've included this squash dish in our sides and lunches section, it makes a perfect meal whatever time of the day you fancy. Easy and quick to make, it's another comfort food dish that will warm you up and leave you feeling satisfied.

Serves: 4

Time: 15 mins

- Calories: 41g
- Net carbs: 8g
- Protein: 2g
- Fat: 1g

Ingredients:

- 3-4 cups cooked spaghetti squash
- 8 pieces cooked bacon, chopped
- 1 ½ cups steamed broccoli

For the sauce...

- 1 cup coconut milk
- 1 medium egg
- 1 teaspoon sea salt
- 1 teaspoon garlic powder
- Fresh ground pepper, to taste

Method:

1. Preheat the oven to 400°F.
2. Place a saucepan over a medium heat, add the sauce ingredients and whisk well.
3. Cook for 5-10 minutes until it becomes thick and delicious.
4. Find a casserole dish, add the cooked spaghetti squash, steamed broccoli and bacon, pour the cream sauce over the top then pop into the oven for a few minutes to keep warm.
5. Serve and enjoy.

Chicken Pesto Stuffed Sweet Potatoes

Stuffed sweet potatoes might take a little while to make but they are seriously amazing. Make ahead if you can and pop into the fridge for a healthy snack, lunch or side dish that will keep you looking and feeling great.

Serves: 6

Time: 1 hour 5 mins

- Calories: 573
- Net carbs: 29g
- Protein: 22g
- Fat: 41g

Ingredients:

For the pesto...

- 1 cup raw shelled walnuts
- 4-5 cloves garlic, chopped
- 3 cups fresh basil leaves
- 2 cups fresh spinach kale, or other leafy greens
- 2/3 cup light olive oil
- 1 1/2-2 tablespoons fresh lemon juice
- 2 tablespoons nutritional yeast
- 3/4 teaspoons sea salt

For the chicken...

- 3 cups cooked shredded chicken breast

For the sweet potatoes...

- 6 medium sweet potatoes
- Coconut oil
- Salt, to taste

Method:

1. Preheat your oven to 400°F and grease a baking sheet.
2. Find a medium bowl, add the coconut oil then sprinkle with salt. Stir well to coat.
3. Place onto the baking sheet and pop into the oven for 60 minutes until cooked.
4. Grab a blender and add the pesto ingredients. Whizz until smooth.
5. Find a large bowl and add the chicken and pesto. Stir well to combine.
6. When the potatoes are ready, slice in half and stuff with the chicken pesto mixture.
7. Serve and enjoy.

Classic Devilled Eggs

Fancy a naughty snack with a clean eating facelift? Yeah, I thought you'd say this. Try these sin-free devilled eggs.

Serves: 10
Time: 5 mins
- Calories: 83g
- Net carbs: 0g
- Protein: 4g
- Fat: 7g

Ingredients:
- 10 hard-boiled eggs, sliced in half lengthways
- 1/4 cup + 1 tablespoon mayonnaise (see recipe here)
- 1/2 teaspoon salt
- 1/2 teaspoon Dijon mustard
- 1 teaspoon yellow mustard
- 1/2 teaspoon white vinegar

To serve...
- Fresh chives, chopped
- Paprika
- Fresh dill, chopped

Method:
1. Remove the egg yolks from the eggs and place into a small bowl.
2. Add the remaining ingredients, mash well then stir to combine.
3. Fill the cooked egg whites with the yolk mixture then sprinkle with the optional toppings.
4. Serve and enjoy.

Spinach Artichoke Twice Baked Potatoes

Creamy and cheesy, these are filling, delicious and perfect for any meal.

Serves: 4

Time: 1 hour 40 mins

- Calories: 364
- Net carbs: 56g
- Protein: 8g
- Fat: 14g

Ingredients:

- 4 medium russet potatoes
- 5 oz. container fresh baby spinach
- 1/2 x 14 oz. can artichoke hearts
- 1/2 medium onion, diced
- 2 cloves garlic minced
- 1 x 5.3 oz. can coconut cream
- 1 ½ tablespoons fresh lemon juice
- 3/4 teaspoons fine grain sea salt
- 2 tablespoons nutritional yeast
- 2 tablespoons ghee

Method:

1. Preheat the oven to 400°F and grease a baking tray.
2. Place the potatoes onto a flat surface, rub with coconut oil and sprinkle with salt.
3. Pop onto a baking tray and place into the oven for around an hour until cooked through.
4. Remove from the oven and leave to cool slightly.
5. Cut each potato lengthwise and scoop out the potato insides. Place into a bowl.
6. Pop a skillet over a medium heat, add a tablespoon of ghee or olive oil then add the onions.
7. Cook for five minutes until soft then add the garlic and cook for another minute.
8. Add the spinach and stir well, allowing to wilt.
9. Add the artichoke and salt then cook for another minute then remove from the heat and pop to one side.
10. Take the bowl with the potato insides and add the coconut cream, lemon juice, nutritional yeast, ghee or coconut oil and the salt. Mash well together.
11. Add the artichoke mixture, stir well then use to fill the potato skins.
12. Pop back into the oven for 15 minutes until brown then serve and enjoy.

Chipotle Chicken Stuffed Sweet Potatoes

Just when you thought that stuffed potatoes couldn't get any better, along I come to give you this chipotle chicken dish. Spicy, creamy and amazing, you have to try it to believe it.

Serves: 4

Time: 1 hour

- Calories: 457
- Net carbs: 26g
- Protein: 26g
- Fat: 24g

Ingredients:

- 4 medium sweet potatoes
- Coconut oil, to taste
- Salt, to taste
- 1 lb. cooked chicken breast, skin removed
- 2 large handfuls kale, chopped
- 1/2 medium onion, chopped
- 2 cloves garlic, minced
- 1 tablespoons ghee, olive oil or coconut oil

For the chipotle sauce...

- 1/3 cup avocado oil or light olive oil
- 2 1/2 tablespoons fresh lime juice
- 2 teaspoons chili powder
- 1/2 teaspoon cumin
- 1/2 teaspoon chipotle powder (or to taste)
- 1/2 teaspoon smoked paprika
- 1/2 teaspoon garlic powder
- 1/4 teaspoon sea salt

For the ranch dressing...

- 1/2 cup mayonnaise (see recipe here)
- 1 teaspoon garlic powder
- 1 teaspoon dried chives
- 1/4 teaspoon dried dill optional
- 1 teaspoon fresh lemon juice
- Salt, to taste

To serve...
- Cilantro
- Ranch dressing

Method:
1. Start by making the ranch dressing. Simply place the ingredients into a bowl, stir well then pop into the fridge.
2. Then preheat the oven to 425°F and grease a baking sheet.
3. Place the potatoes onto a flat surface, pierce with a fork then rub with coconut oil and sprinkle with salt.
4. Place onto the baking tray and pop into the oven for around an hour until cooked through.
5. Pop a skillet over a medium heat, add some coconut oil and add the onion and cook for five minutes until soft.
6. Add the garlic, stir well and cook for another minute.
7. Add the kale, season with salt and leave to cook for a further few minutes. Remove from the heat.
8. Make the chipotle sauce by finding a medium bowl, adding the chipotle ingredients then whisking well.
9. Find a large bowl, add the chicken and shred using two forks.
10. Add the kale mixture then stir well.
11. Pour the sauce over everything and stir again.
12. When the potatoes are ready, remove from the oven and cut lengthways then add the chicken mixture.
13. Serve and enjoy.

Zucchini and Thyme Fritters

Zucchini and thyme come together in these clean-eating fritters which are surprising easy to make, satisfying and work well with salmon, eggs and whatever else you can dream up. Enjoy.

Serves: 8
Time: 30 mins

- Calories: 106
- Net carbs: 2g
- Protein: 4g
- Fat: 9g

Ingredients:

- 2 medium-sized zucchinis, grated
- 2 teaspoons salt
- 2 tablespoons fresh thyme leaves
- 1 teaspoon garlic powder
- 3/4 cup blanched almond meal
- 2 free-range eggs
- Ghee, to taste

To serve...

- Avocado
- Poached egg
- Smoked salmon

Method:

1. Find a large bowl and add the zucchini and salt. Stir well and leave to rest for 10 minutes.
2. Using your hands, squeeze as much of the liquid from the zucchini as you can then place into a bowl.
3. Add the remaining ingredients and stir well to combine.
4. Pop a skillet over a medium heat and add some ghee.
5. Use your hands to form fritters and place into the skillet. Cook until brown.
6. Repeat with the remaining ingredients then serve and enjoy.

Sweet Potato Chicken Poppers

These poppers look so much like 'junk' food that you'll wonder if you dreamed up the recipe. Crunchy, nutritious and very moreish, these are a keeper.

Serves: 4
Time: 45 mins

- Calories: 277
- Net carbs: 18g
- Protein: 27g
- Fat: 10g

Ingredients:

- 1 lb. ground chicken (uncooked)
- 2 cups uncooked sweet potato, finely grated
- 2 tablespoons coconut oil + 1 teaspoon
- 2 tablespoons coconut flour
- 2–3 sprigs green onion, chopped
- 1 tablespoons garlic powder
- 1 tablespoons onion powder
- 1 teaspoon sea salt
- 1/2 teaspoon black pepper
- 1 teaspoon paprika or chili powder (opt.)

Method:

1. Preheat the oven to 400°F and grease a baking sheet.
2. Grab a large mixing bowl and add all the ingredients. Stir well.
3. Use your hands to form the mixture into small nugget shapes and place onto the baking sheet.
4. Pop into the oven for around 30 minutes until crispy and brown.
5. Serve and enjoy.

Tostones with Guacamole

I first tried these crunchy treats when I made friends with a Cuban guy who was a complete foodie and insisted that his tostones were the best in the world. Over the years, I've perfected his recipe to create this. But shhhh...don't tell him!

Serves: 2-4

Time: 20 mins

- Calories: 176
- Net carbs: 18g
- Protein: 2g
- Fat: 8g

Ingredients:

- 3 green plantains, peeled and sliced into 3/4-inch rounds
- 3 cups ghee or olive oil
- 1 large avocado
- 1 tablespoon lime juice
- Salt, to taste

To serve...

- Fresh oregano leaves

Method:

1. Grab a pan that is at least 3 inches deep, add the oil and place over a medium heat.
2. When the oil is hot, add the plantain and fry until golden brown but still slightly soft.
3. Remove from the oil and drain on paper towels.
4. Using the back of a spoon or mason jar, squash each until they're about ¼ inch thick then return to the oil.
5. Fry again until brown and crispy, season well then pop to one side.
6. Grab a medium bowl and add the avocado, lime juice and salt, then serve with the tostones. Enjoy!

Main Meals (Chicken & Turkey)

Coconut Curry Chicken Meatballs

Just when you thought that meatballs couldn't get any better, these awesome curry and lime meatballs come along and blast your taste buds. Simply amazing!

Makes: 20 meatballs

Time: 40 mins

- Calories: 280
- Net carbs: 6g
- Protein: 16g
- Fat: 22g

Ingredients:

For the meatballs...

- 1/2 cup roughly chopped carrots
- 1/4 red onion chopped
- 2 tablespoons cilantro
- Juice 1 lime
- 2 tablespoons basil
- 1 tablespoons coconut aminos
- 1 teaspoon ground ginger
- 1 clove garlic, minced
- 1/2 teaspoon ground cumin
- 1/4 teaspoon red chili flakes
- 1/4 teaspoon sea salt
- ¼ teaspoon pepper
- 1 lb. ground chicken

For the sauce...

- 1 x 14 oz. can coconut milk
- 1 tablespoon red curry paste
- 1 tablespoon almond butter
- 2 tablespoons lime juice
- 1 teaspoon minced garlic

Method:

1. Preheat the oven to 400°F and grease a baking sheet with a small amount of oil.
2. Grab a good processor and place everything except the chicken inside. Whizz until chopped.
3. Add the chicken and stir well.

4. Using your hands, form into medium sized balls and place onto the baking sheet.
5. Pop into the oven for 20 minutes then turn and cook for another 15 mins.
6. Meanwhile, place a large skillet over a medium heat and add the coconut milk.
7. Throw in the remaining ingredients, bring to the boil and simmer for 10 minutes, stirring often.
8. When the meatballs are cooked, transfer to the sauce and warm for another minute or so.
9. Serve and enjoy.

Grilled Chicken Kabobs

These simple chicken kabobs are delicious and work perfectly when served with a side of veggies or when you want something different for your BBQ. If you're using bamboo or wooden skewers, remember to soak them at least 30 minutes before using.

Serves: 4

Time: 20 mins

- Calories: 202
- Net carbs: 2g
- Protein: 33g
- Fat: 8g

Ingredients:

For the paste...

- 1 tablespoon minced garlic
- 1/2 teaspoon fine salt
- 1/2 teaspoon freshly ground pepper
- 2 teaspoons minced fresh oregano
- 1 tablespoon olive oil
- 1 tablespoon lime juice

For the chicken...

- 1 1/2 lb. boneless skinless chicken breast, cut into 1" chunks

Method:

1. Grab a medium bowl and combine the ingredients for the paste. Stir well.
2. Place the chicken into a glass container with a lid, cover with the paste and stir well.
3. Leave to rest in the fridge for at least two hours, preferably overnight.
4. When it's time to cook, preheat your broiler to 350°F.
5. Remove the chicken from the fridge and thread onto the skewers.
6. Place under the broiler and cook for about 10 minutes until the chicken is cooked through.
7. Serve and enjoy.

Healthy Chicken Tenders

If you have kids (and bigger kids) in the family, then they're going to love these healthy and nutritious coconut chicken pieces. Yum!

Serves: 4

Time: 35 mins

- Calories: 295
- Net carbs: 8g
- Protein: 29g
- Fat: 15g

Ingredients:

- 1 lb. chicken tenders
- 1/4 cup shredded unsweetened coconut
- 1/4 cup coconut flour
- 1/2 cup almond meal
- 1 teaspoon pepper
- 1 free-range egg, beaten
- 1 tablespoon almond milk

Method:

1. Preheat your oven to 450°F and grease a baking sheet.
2. Find a small bowl and combine the shredded coconut, coconut flour, almond meal and pepper.
3. Take another bowl and combine one egg and the milk. Whisk well to combine.
4. Dip the chicken into the egg mixture and allow any excess to drip away.
5. Then dip the chicken into the bread and coat completely.
6. Place onto the baking sheet and pop into the oven for 15 minutes until cooked through.
7. Flip, cook for another ten minutes then serve and enjoy.

Greek Chicken Zucchini Noodles

Whether you're looking for a healthy dinner that will be on the table fast or you're craving Greek food or noodles, give these a try. You won't be disappointed.

Serves: 2

Time: 30 mins

- Calories: 545
- Net carbs: 12g
- Protein: 53g
- Fat: 28g

Ingredients:

- 1 tablespoon olive oil
- 1 lb. chicken breasts, cut into ½" cubes
- 1/2 teaspoon pepper
- 1/2 teaspoon oregano dried
- 1/2 teaspoon thyme
- 1/2 teaspoon basil dried
- 1/3 cup kalamata olives, halved
- 1/3 cup sun-dried tomatoes in olive oil, drained
- 1 cup marinated artichoke hearts
- 1 tablespoon lemon juice, freshly squeezed
- 1 lb. zucchini spiralized

Method:

1. Take a skillet, place over a medium heat and add the olive oil.
2. Add the chicken and cook for around 15 minutes until browned on the edges.
3. Add the spices, olives, tomatoes and artichokes and stir to combine. Cook for another 2 minutes.
4. Add the zucchini and lemon juice, toss and serve immediately.

Pesto Baked Chicken

Just because dairy is off the menu, that doesn't mean that you can't eat your favorite pesto chicken. And honestly? I think this clean version is even better than the original.

Serves: 4-6

Time: 30 mins

- Calories: 360
- Net carbs: 4g
- Protein: 5g
- Fat: 38g

Ingredients:

For the pesto...

- 1 cup raw shelled walnuts
- 3 cups fresh basil leaves
- 2 cups fresh baby spinach leaves
- 4 cloves garlic, minced
- 2/3 cup light flavored olive oil
- 3/4 teaspoons salt
- 2 tablespoons nutritional yeast

For the chicken...

- 1 ½ lb. boneless skinless chicken breasts
- Sea salt & pepper, to taste
- 4 slices tomato
- Pinch Italian seasoning
- Pinch nutritional yeast

Method:

1. Preheat your oven to 400°F and grease a baking sheet.
2. Grab your blender and add the ingredients for the pesto. Whizz until smooth then pop into the fridge until needed.
3. Pop the chicken onto the baking sheet, coat with around half of the pesto sauce then top with two tomato slices, a pinch of nutritional yeast and Italian seasoning.
4. Pop into the oven for 30 minutes and cook through.
5. Serve and enjoy.

"Breaded" Chicken Cutlets

Lightly flavored with Italian seasoning, this fast chicken recipe is perfect for picky eaters and those who want something delicious for dinner. If you're like me and you adore spice, feel free to increase the garlic and add a touch of chili powder.

Serves: 6

Time: 15 mins

- Calories: 334
- Net carbs: 4g
- Protein: 29g
- Fat: 21g

Ingredients:

For the chicken...

- 1 ½ lb. boneless skinless chicken breasts, thin sliced

The dry ingredients...

- 1 cup blanched almond flour
- 1/4 cup coconut flour
- 1 1/4 teaspoons fine grain sea salt
- 1/8 teaspoon black pepper
- 2 teaspoons Italian seasoning blend
- 1 teaspoon onion powder
- 1/2 teaspoon garlic powder
- Dash red pepper flakes

For the egg dip...

- 1 free-range egg

For frying...

- 3 tablespoons coconut oil
- 2 tablespoons ghee

Method:

1. Find a shallow bowl and combine all the dry ingredients. Stir well!
2. Find another brown ad add the egg, whisking well.
3. Place a skillet over a medium heat and add three tablespoons of cooking fat.
4. Pop the chicken onto a flat surface and season well.
5. Dip into the egg and allow any excess to drip off then dip into the coating.
6. Transfer to the hot oil and fry.
7. Repeat with the remaining chicken breast slices and cook them until brown.
8. Remove and place onto paper towels to absorb any excess oil.
9. Serve and enjoy.

Instant Pot Sweet and Sour Chicken

OK, so you're going to need you Instant Pot to make this guilt-free dinner of delight, but it's absolutely worth it. If you don't have an Instant Pot don't panic. You can make it just the same on your stove. Just roast the chicken separately whilst you make the sauce then combine.

Serves: 6
Time: 30 mins
- Calories: 290
- Net carbs: 26g
- Protein: 23g
- Fat: 9g

Ingredients:

For the chicken...
- 1 ½ lb. chicken thighs or breasts, boneless and skinless then cut into 2" pieces
- Sea salt and pepper, to serve
- 2 tablespoons coconut oil

For the sauce...
- 1 x 20 oz. can pineapple chunks in 100% juice, fruit and juice separated
- 1/3 cup raw apple cider vinegar
- 1/3 cup Whole30 ketchup (see recipe here)
- 4 cloves garlic, minced
- 1" fresh ginger, minced
- 1 large red bell pepper, cut into 1-2" pieces
- 1/8 teaspoon red pepper flakes
- 1 1/2 tablespoon arrowroot starch or tapioca starch

To serve...
- Sliced green onions
- Toasted sesame seeds

Method:
1. Turn your Instant Pot to sauté and add the coconut oil.
2. Season the chicken with plenty of salt and pepper and place inside the Instant Pot, frying for a few minutes on each side.
3. Meanwhile, take a medium bowl and add all the sauce ingredients except the arrowroot, ¼ cup pineapple juice and the red pepper flakes. Stir well to combine.
4. When the chicken has finished sautéing, pour the sauce into the Instant Pot and bring to simmer.
5. Cover with lid and cook on manual high pressure for five minutes.

6. Do a quick pressure release and carefully open the lid.
7. Take a small bowl, add the arrowroot and the ¼ cup pineapple juice then stir well until combined.
8. Turn the Instant Pot onto sauté mode and cook for 5 minutes until the sauce starts to thicken.
9. Cancel and leave to cool for a few minutes before serving and enjoying.

Ginger Lime Sheet Pan Chicken

This has to be one of the easiest dinners on the planet. Simple, tasty and nourishing. What could be better?

Serves: 4
Time: 40 mins

- Calories: 325
- Net carbs: 10g
- Protein: 29g
- Fat: 17g

Ingredients:

- 1 lb. chicken breasts, pounded until thin
- 1 lb. brussels sprouts, halved
- 1 x 10 oz. bag Path of Life Roasted Garlic Cauliflower

For the marinade...

- ¼ cup lime juice
- 1/4 cup olive oil
- 1 tablespoon lime zest
- 1 tablespoon coconut aminos
- 1 teaspoon fresh grated ginger
- ½ teaspoon pepper
- ¼ teaspoon garlic powder

Method:

1. Find a large bowl and add the marinade ingredients. Stir well.
2. Place the chicken into the marinade, stir well to coat and leave to rest for at least 30 minutes, preferably overnight.
3. When you're almost ready to cook, preheat the oven to 450°F and grease a baking sheet.
4. Add the Brussel sprouts to the chicken then transfer to the baking sheet.
5. Pop into the oven for 20 minutes and cook until looking delicious.
6. Add the cauliflower to the baking sheet and pop under the broiler for around 3 minutes.
7. Serve and enjoy.

Chicken Satay with Sunbutter Sauce

This chicken satay tastes like a gift from the sunflower butter gods. Perfectly cooked and with just the right combination of curry, ginger, garlic and crunch, it's a recipe I find myself making at least once per week. The kids love it! Remember to soak your skewers for at least 30 minutes before using.

Serves: 6

Time: 45 mins

- Calories: 248
- Net carbs: 8g
- Protein: 26g
- Fat: 14g

Ingredients:

For the marinade...

- 1 cup full fat coconut milk
- 1 tablespoon curry powder
- 1 teaspoon ginger powder
- 1 tablespoon garlic oil
- 1 teaspoon salt

For the chicken...

- 1 1/2 lb. chicken breast, cut into 1" strips

For the sauce...

- 1/2 cup sugar free sunbutter
- 2 tablespoons coconut aminos
- 1/3 cup warm water
- 1/2 tablespoon hot sauce
- 1 tablespoon garlic oil
- Juice 1 lime

Method:

1. Find a medium bowl and add the marinade ingredients. Stir well to combine.
2. Add the chicken and stir again to coat.
3. Leave to marinade for at least 30 minutes, preferably overnight.
4. Meanwhile, find another bowl and add the ingredients for the sauce. Stir well to combine then pop into the fridge until needed.
5. Preheat the broiler then skewer the chicken.
6. Cook under the broiler for around 5 minutes per side until perfectly done.
7. Serve and enjoy.

Crispy Baked Buffalo Chicken Wings

This chicken wing recipe might seem like it's crazy complicated but it's not that bad. Besides it's absolutely worth it. Perfectly crispy with just the right amount of spice and a creamy and delicious dip, it hits all the right spots.

Serves: 4
Time: 1 hour

- Calories: 422
- Net carbs: 4g
- Protein: 22g
- Fat: 34g

Ingredients:

- 2 lb. chicken wings
- 2 tablespoons arrowroot starch
- 1/2 teaspoon garlic powder
- 1/2 teaspoon onion powder
- 1/4 teaspoon sea salt
- 1/4 teaspoon red cayenne pepper

For the hot dip...

- 1/3 cup ghee, melted
- 1/3 cup + 2 tablespoons hot sauce

For the dip...

- 1/2 cup mayonnaise
- 3 tablespoons coconut cream
- 1/2 teaspoon garlic powder
- 1/2 teaspoon onion powder
- 2 teaspoons dried chives
- 1/4 teaspoon dried dill
- 3/4 teaspoons fresh lemon juice
- 1/8-1/4 teaspoon salt or to taste

Method:

1. Preheat the oven to 425°F then line a baking sheet with foil and place a wire rack over the top.
2. Place the chicken wings into the large bowl and cover with the arrowroot, garlic, onion, salt and red pepper and toss well to coat.
3. Pop the wings onto the wire rack and place into the oven.
4. Cook for 35 minutes.

5. Meanwhile, make the sauce by combining the hot sauce and ghee in a bowl then stirring well.
6. Dip the chicken into the sauce then return to the wire rack.
7. Turn the oven up to 450°F then pop the chicken back into the oven and cook for 10 minutes.
8. Remove from the oven, drizzle with the remaining sauce then bake for five more minutes.
9. Meanwhile, place the ranch dressing ingredients into a bowl, whisk well then serve.
10. Enjoy!

Kung Pao Chicken Wings

Try these Asian-style chicken wings and you'll never go back to the regular kind. Boasting the perfect balance of spicy and salty, they'll wake your taste buds up and keep you fueled all day long.

Serves: 6

Time: 45 mins

- Calories: 399
- Net carbs: 7g
- Protein: 15g
- Fat: 14g

Ingredients:

For the chicken wings...

- 2 ½ lb. split chicken wings
- 2 tablespoons avocado or olive oil
- 1 teaspoon salt
- 1/2 teaspoon pepper

For the sauce...

- 1/4 cup coconut aminos
- 1 teaspoon fish sauce
- 1 teaspoon rice vinegar
- 1 teaspoon freshly grated ginger
- 1/2 teaspoon arrowroot flour
- 2 cloves garlic, finely chopped
- ½-1 teaspoon crushed red pepper
- 2 tablespoons water

To serve...

- 1/4 cup roasted and salted cashews, chopped
- 2 tablespoons green onion (opt.)

Method:

1. Preheat oven to 400°F and grease a baking sheet.
2. Grab a medium bowl and add the chicken wings, avocado oil, salt and pepper. Stir well to combine.
3. Place the chicken wings onto a baking sheet and cook for about 35 minutes until brown.
4. Find a small bowl and combine the sauce ingredients. Whisk well.
5. When the wings have been cooking for about 20 minutes, place a small pan over a medium heat and add the sauce.

6. Cook for about 3 minutes, cooking often until the sauce thickens.
7. Turn heat to low, add water to taste and remove from the heat.
8. Remove the chicken wings from the oven and place into a large bowl.
9. Add the sauce, toss to coat then serve with optional extras. Enjoy.

Lemon Rosemary Chicken Thighs

Another easy sheet pan recipe, these lemon rosemary chicken thighs are simple, ready fast and provide an entire meal in one go. Delicious!

Serves: 2

Time: 30 mins

- Calories: 1119
- Net carbs: 34g
- Protein: 48g
- Fat: 60g

Ingredients:

- 1 1/4 lb. chicken thighs, boned and skinned
- 3 cups brussels sprouts, halved
- 2 cups fingerling potatoes

For the marinade...

- ⅓ cup olive oil
- 1 1/2 tablespoons lemon zest
- ¼ cup lemon juice, freshly squeezed
- ½ tablespoon rosemary, chopped
- 1 teaspoon garlic powder
- 1 teaspoon onion powder
- 1 teaspoon pepper
- ½ teaspoon salt

Method:

1. Preheat the oven to 400°F and grease a baking sheet.
2. Find a medium bowl and add the marinade ingredients. Stir well to coat then leave for at least 30 minutes, preferably overnight.
3. When ready to cook, place the chicken thighs onto the baking sheet, keeping the leftover marinade in the dish.
4. Add the Brussel sprouts and potatoes to the marinade and toss well until coated.
5. Place the Brussel sprouts onto the baking sheet with the chicken and pop it into the oven.
6. Bake for 20 minutes until crisp.

Crockpot Turkey Chili

Yes, there might be a long list of ingredients here, but I promise that it's not so bad. Besides, the result is very much worth it. If you don't own a crockpot, feel free to cook on the stove and for extra time savings, use cooked turkey. You're welcome.

Serves: 6

Time: 6 hours 30 mins

- Calories: 231
- Net carbs: 14g
- Protein: 29g
- Fat: 6g

Ingredients:

- 2 lb. ground turkey
- 2 tablespoons olive oil
- 1 cup onion, minced
- 1 tablespoon garlic, minced
- 1 cup peppers, chopped in small pieces
- 1 cup carrots, chopped in small pieces
- 40 oz. canned crushed tomatoes
- 1 tablespoon paprika
- 1/4 teaspoon red pepper flakes
- 1 teaspoon pepper
- 2 teaspoons chili powder
- 1 teaspoon cumin
- 1/2 teaspoon salt
- 1/4 teaspoon cinnamon
- 1/2 teaspoon turmeric
- 2 cups steamed sweet potato noodles or cauliflower rice

Method:

1. Find a medium skillet, place over a medium heat and add the oil.
2. Add the turkey and cook for about 10 minutes until browned.
3. Transfer the turkey to the crockpot with the remaining ingredients.
4. Cover with the lid and cook on low for 6 hours until tender and fragrant.
5. Serve and enjoy.

Turkey Mushroom Apple Stuffed Acorn Squash

When you see this stuffed squash on your dinner plate, you'll be forgiven for thinking that it's a complicated dish that will take your hours. But actually, it's pretty fast and well worth the results.

Serves: 4

Time: 1 hour

- Calories: 429
- Net carbs: 26g
- Protein: 37g
- Fat: 19g

Ingredients:

- 2 acorn squash, halved
- 2 tablespoons olive oil
- 1 lb. ground turkey
- 1 1/2 cups baby Bella mushrooms, chopped
- 1 cup honey crisp apples, peeled chopped in small pieces
- 1/2 cup chicken stock
- 2 teaspoon fresh rosemary, chopped finely
- 1 teaspoon pepper
- 1/2 teaspoon salt
- 1 teaspoon garlic powder
- 1 teaspoon onion powder
- Nutritional yeast, to taste

Method:

1. Preheat your oven to 450°F and grease a baking sheet.
2. Place the acorn squash onto the baking sheet and pop into the oven for 20 minutes until tender.
3. Meanwhile, grab a skillet, place over a medium heat and add the oil.
4. Cook the turkey for 10 minutes until brown, stirring often.
5. Add the mushrooms, apples, chicken stock and spices to the pan with the turkey and cook for another five minutes.
6. Remove the squash from the oven and scoop out most of the cooked flesh from the center (but keep the skin for stuffing).
7. Add the flesh to the turkey in the pan and stir through well.
8. Take the skin from the squash and fill with the turkey mixture.
9. Pop into the oven for 10 minutes until browned and looking delicious.
10. Sprinkle with nutritional yeast then serve and enjoy.

Main Meals (Pork)

Zucchini Carbonara

Hand up if you'd love to enjoy a creamy, tasty carbonara right now...Oh yeah me too! I love this zucchini version as it's super low carb, packed with healthy vitamins, minerals and antioxidants and doesn't sit in my stomach like a lead weight.

Serves: 4

Time: 30 mins

- Calories: 316
- Net carbs: 6g
- Protein: 12g
- Fat: 26g

Ingredients:

- 3-4 medium zucchini, spiralized
- 1 teaspoon salt

For the bacon...

- 6 slices sugar-free bacon, cut into small pieces
- 3 cloves garlic, minced

For the sauce...

- 2 large free-range eggs
- 2-3 tablespoons nutritional yeast
- 1/2 teaspoon arrowroot starch
- 1/4 teaspoon fine grain sea salt
- 1/4 teaspoon black pepper
- 1/2 cup coconut cream

To serve...

- Chopped parsley
- Crushed red pepper

Method:

1. Find a colander and place over a large bowl.
2. Add the zucchini, sprinkle with salt and leave for 30 minutes to draw out the water.
3. Squeeze out any remaining liquid then pop onto paper towels.
4. Find a medium bowl and combine the sauce ingredients, except the coconut milk. Stir well to combine.
5. Find a small saucepan, place over a medium heat and add the coconut cream.
6. Whisk until melted then add the egg mixture and whisk again.
7. Remove from the heat and pop to one side.
8. Next place a skillet over a medium heat and add the bacon. Cook until brown.

82

9. Remove and place onto a paper towel. Retain a tablespoon of the bacon fat and turn the heat down.
10. Add the garlic to the pan and cook for 30 seconds until softening.
11. Throw in the zucchini, toss well then raise heat to medium.
12. Serve and enjoy.

Instant Pot Jamaican Jerk Pork Roast

This Jamaican pork is so easy, so delicious and so versatile that it's worth making a batch of this and using throughout the week as your meal prep. You'll need an Instant Pot to do it quickly, but you can also do it in your oven if required.

Serves: 12

Time: 1 hour

- Calories: 282
- Net carbs: 0g
- Protein: 23g
- Fat: 20g

Ingredients:

- 4 lb. pork shoulder
- 1/4 cup Jamaican Jerk spice blend (sugar free)
- 1 tablespoons olive oil
- 1/2 cup beef stock or broth

Method:

1. Place the roast onto a flat surface, rub with olive oil and coat with the spice blend.
2. Turn the Instant Pot onto sauté, add the meat and brown on all sides.
3. Add the broth then cover with the lid.
4. Cook on manual high pressure for 45 minutes.
5. Do a quick pressure release then carefully open the lid.
6. Shred using two forks then serve and enjoy.

Garlic Lime Pork Chops

Fast and delicious, these ginger lime chops taste great served with a side of salad or whatever veggie your heart desires.

Serves: 4
Time: 30 mins

- Calories: 224
- Net carbs: 2g
- Protein: 38g
- Fat: 6g

Ingredients:

- 4 x 6 oz. each boneless pork chops
- 4 cloves garlic, crushed
- 1/2 teaspoon cumin
- 1/2 teaspoon chili powder
- 1/2 teaspoon paprika
- Juice of ½ lime
- 1 teaspoon lime zest
- Salt and pepper, to taste

Method:

1. Find a large bowl and add all the ingredients. Stir well to combine.
2. Leave to marinade for at least 20 minutes.
3. Preheat the broiler and cover the bottom of the pan with foil.
4. Broil the pork chops for about 5 minutes on each side then leave to rest for a minute or two.
5. Serve and enjoy.

Creamy & Smoky Chipotle Pork Chops

Words aren't enough for these amazing pork chops. If you only make one pork recipe in this entire book, make sure it's this one.

Serves: 5
Time: 20 mins

- Calories: 125
- Net carbs: 4g
- Protein: 6g
- Fat: 11g

Ingredients:

- 4-5 boneless center cut pork chops
- 2 tablespoons olive oil

For the rub...

- 1 tablespoon chili powder
- 1 teaspoon paprika
- 1/2 teaspoon cumin
- 1/2 teaspoon chipotle chili pepper
- 1/2 teaspoon coarse sea salt
- 1 cloves garlic, minced

For the sauce...

- 1 cup canned coconut milk
- 1/2 teaspoon chipotle chili pepper
- 1 teaspoon liquid smoke
- 1/4 cup chopped fresh cilantro

For garnish...

- Juice 1 lime
- Chopped fresh cilantro

Method:

1. Find a medium bowl, add the ingredients for the rub and stir well to combine.
2. Take your pork chops, rub with the oil then toss into the rub.
3. Place large skillet over a medium heat and add the olive oil.
4. Cook the pork shops for 5 minutes on each side until cooked.
5. Take a food processor and add the sauce ingredients. Whizz until smooth.
6. Pour the sauce over the pork chops and then reduce the heat to low.
7. Simmer until the sauce reduces slightly reduces then serve and enjoy.

Egg Roll in a Bowl with Creamy Chili Sauce

Can you believe how moreish this recipe is?? Just one bit is all it will take for you to get head over heels addicted with the perfect combo of flavors. Wow.

Serves: 4

Time: 25 mins

- Calories: 416
- Net carbs: 12g
- Protein: 10g
- Fat: 21g

Ingredients:

- 2 tablespoons sesame oil
- 6 green onions sliced, green and white parts divided
- 1/2 cup red onion, diced
- 5 cloves garlic, minced
- 1 lb. ground pork
- 1 teaspoon fresh grated ginger
- 1 x 8 oz. can water chestnuts, chopped
- 1 tablespoon sriracha or hot sauce
- 1 x 14 oz. bag coleslaw mix
- 3 tablespoons coconut aminos
- 1 tablespoon rice wine vinegar
- Salt and pepper, to taste

For the creamy sauce...

- 1/4 cup mayonnaise (see recipe here)
- 1-2 tablespoons sriracha or hot sauce salt, to taste

Method:

1. Place a skillet over a medium heat and add the sesame oil.
2. Add the red onion, green onion and garlic and cook for five minutes until soft.
3. Add the pork, ginger, chestnuts and hot sauce and cook until the pork is cooked through.
4. Add the remaining ingredients, stir well then cook until the cabbage is tender.
5. Meanwhile, find a medium bowl and add the creamy sauce ingredients. Stir well until combined.
6. Serve and enjoy.

Coriander Lime Pork Chops with Peppers and Onions

Let's be honest. You really can't go wrong with coriander, lime and pork, can you? Whip it all up with bags of spice and serve with a creamy avocado and you'll be fueled and satisfied.

Serves: 4
Time: 30 mins

- Calories: 241
- Net carbs: 10g
- Protein: 22g
- Fat: 4g

Ingredients:

- 2 red peppers sliced
- 2 1/2 cups sliced red onion
- ½ teaspoons sweet paprika
- ¼ teaspoons red pepper flakes
- ¼ teaspoons chili powder
- ½ teaspoons salt
- 2 large garlic cloves, minced
- 2 tablespoons apple cider vinegar
- 2 tablespoons olive oil

For the pork chops...

- 1 teaspoon salt
- ½ teaspoons pepper
- 2 tablespoons olive oil
- 4 boneless pork chops, ¾ -1″ thick
- 2 tablespoons olive oil

For the sauce...

- 1 tablespoons lime zest
- 2 tablespoons lime juice
- 1 teaspoon coriander powder
- 2 tablespoons ghee or olive oil

For the avocado salsa...

- 1-2 large avocados, cut into chunks
- 2 tablespoons lime juice
- 4 tablespoons chopped cilantro
- Pinch of salt

Method:

1. Place the pork onto a flat surface, season well with salt and pepper and pop to one side.
2. Find a medium bowl and add the avocado, lime, cilantro and salt. Pop to one side.
3. Place a skillet over a medium heat, add 2 tablespoons of oil and add the onions and peppers. Cook for five minutes until soft.
4. Add the paprika, red pepper flake, chili powder, garlic, salt and vinegar.
5. Sook for another five minutes then place into a separate bowl.
6. Wipe the pan then add another 2 tablespoons of oil and place back over the heat.
7. Add the pork and cook on a medium heat and cook for 5-10 minutes until cooked through.
8. Remove from the pan and pop to one side.
9. Next add the ghee, lime zest and juice and ground coriander. Stir and cook for about 30 seconds.
10. Throw the peppers and onions back into the pan and stir well.
11. Add the pork back to the pan and toss well until coated in the sauce.
12. Serve and enjoy.

Polish Pork Cutlets

It's hard to know how to do these delicious pork chops justice using words alone. You really do need to try them. Comforting, crispy and perfectly seasoned with a tender inside, they're fantastic for any meal and keep brilliantly in the fridge if you're doing meal prep.

Serves: 8
Time: 30 mins
- Calories: 354
- Net carbs: 6g
- Protein: 36g
- Fat: 19g

Ingredients:
- 8 pork cutlets
- 1/4 cup tapioca starch
- 2 free-range eggs
- 1 1/2 cups almond flour
- 2 teaspoons salt
- 1 teaspoon pepper
- 1 1/2 teaspoons dill weed
- 1 teaspoon paprika
- 1 teaspoon garlic powder
- 2 tablespoons olive oil
- 2 tablespoons fresh dill

Method:
1. Preheat the oven to 400°F.
2. Find three plates then place the tapioca starch to the first, the eggs into the second and the almond flour and seasonings to the third.
3. Place a skillet over a medium heat and add the oil.
4. Take each pork cutlet and place into the tapioca. Coat well.
5. Dip into the second and allow any excess to drip off.
6. Finally dip into the almond flour and seasoning mixture and shake off the excess.
7. Place into the hot oil into the pan and repeat with the rest.
8. Cook for 3-5 minutes on each side then serve and enjoy!

Main Meals (Beef)

Teriyaki Meatballs

Not only are these meatballs absolutely incredible, the sauce is pretty damn awesome too and works great with any other wholefood dish of your choosing. Just try it and you'll see. Serve with cauliflower rice and broccoli for best results.

Serves: 6
Time: 25 mins
- Calories: 377
- Net carbs: 15g
- Protein: 22g
- Fat: 24g

Ingredients:
- 1 tablespoons coconut oil
- 1 lb. ground beef
- 1/2 lb. ground pork
- 1 large free-range egg
- 1 tablespoons coconut aminos
- 3 tablespoons blanched almond flour
- 1/2-3/4 teaspoons sea salt
- 1/8-1/4 teaspoon black pepper
- 1 teaspoon garlic powder
- 1/2 teaspoon ground ginger

For the sauce...
- 3 Medjool dates, pitted
- 1 1/2 cups very hot water
- 1/2 cup coconut aminos
- 3 cloves garlic, cut into pieces
- 1" fresh ginger, cut into pieces
- 1 tablespoons rice vinegar or apple cider vinegar
- 1 tablespoons tapioca flour

To serve...
- Lots of sliced green onions

Method:
1. Place the dates into a bowl and add enough hot water to cover. Leave to soak for 2 minutes.
2. Grab your food processor and add the dates and water. Whizz until smooth.

91

3. Throw in the remaining sauce ingredients and whizz again.
4. Add the tapioca starch then blend again. Pop to one side.
5. Find a large bowl and add the meatball ingredients (except the green onions). Mix well using your hands.
6. Find a skillet, add the coconut oil and place over a medium heat.
7. Using your hands, shape the mixture into meatballs and place into the pan.
8. Cook for a few minutes until browned.
9. Add the sauce, stir well then lower the heat.
10. Simmer and cook for 10 minutes until the meatballs cooked through.
11. Serve and enjoy.

Real Food Meatloaf

There's nothing quite as comforting as tucking into homemade meatloaf, especially when you know it's super good for you. Made with 100% healthy ingredients, sugar free and packed with taste, it's perfect for anyone who needs a huge from the inside.

Serves: 6-8

Time: 1 hour 20 mins

- Calories: 452
- Net carbs: 80g
- Protein: 20g
- Fat: 7g

Ingredients:

For the ketchup...

- 1/3 cup Medjool dates pitted, soaked in hot water to soften, and drained
- 6 oz. tomato paste
- 3 tablespoons water
- 2 tablespoons raw apple cider vinegar
- 1/2 teaspoon paprika
- 1/2 teaspoon onion powder
- 1/2 teaspoon garlic powder
- 1/2 teaspoon salt
- 1/4 teaspoon chipotle pepper (opt.)

For the meatloaf...

- 2 lb. ground beef
- 2 free-range eggs
- 1/3 cup almond flour
- 3 tablespoons ketchup (see recipe above)
- 1 small onion, minced
- 3 garlic cloves, minced
- 2 tablespoons ghee
- 1 teaspoon salt
- 2 teaspoons mustard
- 1 teaspoon Italian seasoning
- 1/8 teaspoon black pepper

To coat...

- 1/4-1/3 cups ketchup (see the recipe again)

To serve...

- Chopped parsley

Method:

1. Find a food processor and add the ketchup ingredients. Whizz then store in the fridge until needed.
2. Preheat the oven to 375°F and place a skillet over a medium heat.
3. Add oil to the skillet then when hot, add the onions. Cook for five minutes until soft.
4. Add the garlic and a pinch of salt, then cook for another minute. Remove from the heat.
5. Take a large bowl and add the meatloaf ingredients. Mix using your hands.
6. Grab a 9 x 5" loaf pan and transfer the meatloaf ingredients to this pan.
7. Pop into the oven and bake for 20 minutes.
8. Remove from the oven and spread the ketchup to coat over the top.
9. Pop back in the oven and cook for another 40-45 minutes.
10. Remove from the oven, rest for 10 minutes then serve and enjoy.

Thai Red Beef Curry

This effortless beef curry takes just a handful of ingredients and plenty of patience if you cook it the traditional way in an oven. If you can't wait two hours whilst it cooks, feel free to recreate the recipe on your stove or pre-cook the beef.

Serves: 4

Time: 2 hours 15 mins

- Calories: 656
- Net carbs: 1.2g
- Protein: 83g
- Fat: 33g

Ingredients:

- 2 1/2 lb. pastured chuck steak, cubed
- 2 tablespoons sugar-free Thai red curry paste
- 1/4 cup beef bone broth, warmed
- 1 teaspoon turmeric powder
- 1 x 14 oz. can coconut cream
- Zest and juice from 1/2 lime
- 3/4 teaspoons salt

Method:

1. Preheat the oven to 425°F.
2. Find a large bowl and add the curry paste, turmeric, salt, lime juice and zest and broth. Stir well to combine.
3. Add the meat and coconut cream and stir through well.
4. Place into an ovenproof dish and then cover with the lid.
5. Pop into the oven and cook for 2 hours.
6. Remove from the oven, stir then pop it back in for an hour. Cook until the meat is falling off the bone.
7. Remove from the oven then place all the meat pieces into a bowl. Pop to one side.
8. Transfer the juices to a saucepan, turn up the heat and reduce until it thickens.
9. Serve the meat with the sauce and enjoy.

Spaghetti Squash with Beef Sauce

Spaghetti bolognaise a la gluten free, sugar-free and healthy? Oooh I don't mind if I do.

Serves: 2

Time: 50 mins

- Calories: 443
- Net carbs: 29g
- Protein: 34g
- Fat: 36g

Ingredients:

- 1 large or 2 small spaghetti squashes, sliced lengthways and seeds removed
- 2-4 fresh rosemary sprigs
- 1/2 lb. ground beef
- 1 1/2 tablespoons grass-fed ghee, divided
- 1 scallion, thinly sliced
- 1 leek, thinly sliced
- 1 teaspoon dried thyme
- 1 1/2 teaspoons dried oregano
- 14 oz. tomato passata

To serve...

- Handful of fresh basil and flat leaf parsley leaves
- 1 tablespoon extra-virgin olive oil

Method:

1. Preheat the oven to 350°F and grease a baking sheet.
2. Place rosemary on the tray, place the squash face down on the baking sheet and then pop into the oven.
3. Bake for 30 minutes until tender.
4. Meanwhile, place a pan over a medium heat and add the ghee.
5. Add the leeks and cook for five minutes until soft.
6. Add the beef and herbs and cook for a few minutes until brown.
7. Add the tomato, stir well then bring to a light boil.
8. Reduce the heat and cook for 20 minutes.
9. Remove the squash from the oven, cook for five minutes then scrape the flesh from the squash.
10. Divide the squash between two plates, top with the meat sauce then serve and enjoy.

Crockpot Meatballs in Marinara Sauce

Perfect for lazy Sundays or any family gathering, these meatballs are easy to throw together and leave to cook whilst you get on having fun.

Serves: 8
Time: 4 hours 15 mins

- Calories: 327
- Net carbs: 8g
- Protein: 20g
- Fat: 22g

Ingredients:

- 1 3/4 lb. ground beef
- 1 free-range egg
- 1/4 cup blanched almond flour
- 3/4 teaspoons fine grain sea salt, divided
- 2 teaspoons onion powder
- 1/2 teaspoon garlic powder
- 1 tablespoon Italian seasoning blend
- Pinch crushed red pepper, to taste
- 1 tablespoon chopped fresh parsley
- 28 oz. can crushed tomatoes with basil
- 14 oz. can diced tomatoes with basil and garlic
- 1 x 6 oz. can tomato paste
- 1/2 medium onion, chopped
- 2 tablespoons chopped fresh garlic
- 2 tablespoons chopped fresh oregano leaves
- 2 bay leaves
- Sea salt, to taste

Method:

1. Take a bowl and add the almond flour, ½ teaspoon of sea salt, onion, garlic, Italian seasoning and red pepper. Stir well to combine.
2. Find another bowl and add the ground beef and salt.
3. Add the almond flour mix and egg then use your hands to combine.
4. Preheat the broiler and line a baking sheet with parchment paper.
5. Use your hands to form the mixture into meatballs then pop onto the baking sheet.
6. Pop under the broiler for 5 minutes and brown, turning often.
7. Add the meatballs to your crockpot, top with the sauce and stir well.
8. Cover and cook on low for 4 hours.
9. Serve and enjoy.

Salisbury Steak Meatballs

Yes, this is another recipe for meatballs and no, they're nothing like the other ones we've included in this book. Flecked with mushrooms, steak, mustard and garlic and with a mouthwatering smokey taste, they're something special for when you most deserve it.

Serves: 6

Time: 30 mins

- Calories: 371
- Net carbs: 7g
- Protein: 24g
- Fat: 26g

Ingredients:

For the meatballs...

- 1 1/2 lb. ground beef
- 1 free-range egg
- 1/3 cup blanched almond flour
- 3/4 teaspoons fine grain sea salt
- 1/4 teaspoon black pepper
- 2 tablespoons tomato paste
- 2 tablespoons brown mustard
- 1 teaspoon garlic powder
- 2 teaspoons onion powder
- 1 tablespoons coconut aminos
- 1/4 teaspoon liquid smoke (opt.)
- 1 cup white mushrooms, divided (1/4 cup finely chopped)
- 1 tablespoons ghee
- Parsley chopped, for garnish

For the sauce...

- 12 oz. beef bone broth divided (1 cup + 1/2 cup)
- 1 tablespoons ghee
- 1 medium onion, chopped
- 3 cloves garlic, chopped
- 1 tablespoons arrowroot powder or tapioca
- 1 teaspoon mustard
- 2 teaspoons coconut aminos

Method:

1. Grab a large bowl and add the meatball ingredients.
2. Using your hands, stir well and form into meatballs.

3. Place a skillet over a medium heat, add a tablespoon of the ghee and then add the meatballs.
4. Cook for 5 minutes or so, turning often.
5. Add another tablespoon of ghee to the pan and add the onions. Cook for five minutes until soft.
6. Add the garlic and cook for another minute.
7. Add a cup of the bone broth then the mustard, aminos and sliced mushrooms.
8. Bring to a simmer and stir well.
9. Find a small bowl and add the arrowroot and the remaining broth. Stir well to combine and then add to the pan.
10. Add the meatballs to the pan, cover with the lid and simmer on low for 5-10 minutes.
11. Serve and enjoy.

Instant Pot Beef Chili with Bacon

Nothing like a well-rounded beef chili to fill you up, warm you from the inside out and keep you on your toes. Fill up with this one and you're sure to be feeling satisfied.

Serves: 10

Time: 45 mins

- Calories: 313
- Net carbs: 7g
- Protein: 17g
- Fat: 23g

Ingredients:

- 1 1/2 lb. ground beef grass fed
- 1/2 lb. sugar-free bacon, cut into pieces
- 1 medium onion, chopped
- 1 large red bell pepper, chopped
- 2 small jalapeno peppers, seeded and minced
- 3 cloves garlic, minced
- 1 x 28 oz. can diced tomatoes
- 6 oz. can tomato paste
- 12 oz. bone broth beef
- 1 teaspoon cumin
- 1 teaspoon smoked paprika
- 1 tablespoon chili powder
- 1/2 teaspoon chipotle powder
- 1 teaspoon fine grain sea salt

To serve...

- Cilantro
- Lime
- Avocado, sliced

Method:

1. Grab your Instant Pot and turn onto sauté.
2. Add the bacon and cook until crisp. Remove from the pan and pop to one side.
3. Retain a tablespoon of the fat but discard the rest.
4. Add the beef to the pan and cook until brown, stirring often.
5. Once the beef is almost done, add the veggies and cook until tender.
6. Add the remaining ingredients, cover with the id and then cook on manual high pressure for 10 minutes.
7. Do a quick pressure release, add the bacon and then stir well.
8. Leave to cool for a few minutes then serve and enjoy.

Crockpot Beef Stew

No beef section would be complete without a great recipe for one of my favorite easy dishes- beef stew. It's simple, you probably have most of the ingredients in your pantry already and you can throw in whatever veggies you have to hand. Enjoy!

Serves: 7-8

Time: 8 hours

- Calories: 553
- Net carbs: 5g
- Protein: 17g
- Fat: 37g

Ingredients:

- 3 1/2 lb. beef, diced
- 1 1/2 cups beef bone broth
- 3 stalks celery, chopped
- 3 carrots, chopped into large rounds
- 1 tablespoon chopped ginger
- 3 garlic cloves, minced
- 1 leek, white part only
- 1 x 15 oz. can diced tomatoes
- 3 handfuls fresh spinach
- 2 tablespoons apple cider vinegar
- 2 teaspoons dried rosemary
- 2 teaspoons dried thyme
- 2 teaspoons dried oregano
- 1 tablespoon grass-fed ghee or coconut oil
- Salt and pepper, to taste

Method:

1. Take a skillet, pop over a medium heat and add the ghee.
2. When the oil is hot add the beef and cook until brown.
3. Place the beef into the crockpot.
4. Add the remaining ingredients (except the spinach) and stir well to combine.
5. Cook on low for 5-8 hours.
6. Open the lid, add the spinach and stir through.
7. Serve and enjoy.

Asian Beef and Broccoli

Love beef? Love broccoli? Love Asian flavors? Then I know the perfect recipe for you...

Serves: 4

Time: 35 mins

- Calories: 340
- Net carbs: 11g
- Protein: 25g
- Fat: 10g

Ingredients:

- ¾ lb. lean steak, thinly sliced
- 2 tablespoons arrowroot or cornstarch
- 1 lb. broccoli, cut into 2" sections
- 1/2 cup coconut aminos, or soy sauce
- 3 cloves garlic, minced
- 1 1/2 teaspoons fresh ginger, minced
- 1/2 teaspoon black pepper
- 1/4–1/2 cup water, as desired
- Olive oil or coconut oil, for cooking

Method:

1. Take a medium bowl and add the steak, arrowroot and a pinch of pepper. Stir well to coat.
2. Place a skillet over a medium heat and add some oil.
3. When the oil is hot, add the steak to the pan and cook for a minute or so on each side. Pop to one side.
4. Add the broccoli to the pan and cook for five minutes until tender. Pop to one side.
5. Take a medium bowl and add the aminos, garlic, ginger and pepper. Stir well.
6. Pour the sauce into the pan and heat gentle until it starts to reduce. Add water if required.
7. Serve together and enjoy.

Main Meals (Lamb)

Lamb & Mint Chimichurri & Butternut "Rice"

Words aren't enough for this delicious recipe. Combining tasty chimichurri, tender lamb and perfectly sweet butternut squash, this is certainly a dish to remember. Serve it when you've got guests coming over and they're sure to go wild.

Serves: 4

Time: 40 mins

- Calories: 623
- Net carbs: 43g
- Protein: 41g
- Fat: 23g

Ingredients:

- 2 lb. boneless lamb loin
- Salt and pepper, to taste
- 1 tablespoon olive oil

For the chimichurri...

- 1 cup firmly packed fresh mint leaves
- ½ cup firmly packed flat-leaf parsley
- 2 garlic cloves, chopped
- 1 teaspoon dried crushed red pepper
- ½ cup olive oil
- ⅓ cup red wine vinegar

For the squash ....

- 1 butternut squash, peeled, seeded and roughly chopped
- 1 tablespoon ghee
- 3 cups beef broth

Method:

1. Preheat your broiler to 400°F.
2. Grab a food processor, add the chimichurri ingredients then hit whizz until blended.
3. Pour into a bowl then pop to one side.
4. Rinse the food processor bowl then add the squash, blend until it's chopped into 'rice' and pop to one side.
5. Place the lamb into the broiler tray and cook for 5 minutes on each side until cooked.
6. Remove from the broiler, cover with foil and leave to rest for 7 minutes until cooked through.

7. Find a medium pan, cover with the broth (just enough so it's covered) then pop over a medium heat.

8. Bring to the boil then reduce the heat and simmer for 7 minutes until the squash has cooked through. Drain once cooked.

9. Place the lamb onto a chopping board, chop into slices then drizzle with the chimichurri.

10. Serve and enjoy.

Simple Lamb Curry

If you don't want to be spending tons of food but you want to keep it healthy, try out this super-fast, tasty lamb curry.

Serves: 4
Time: 20 mins

- Calories: 463
- Net carbs: 29g
- Protein: 21g
- Fat: 31g

Ingredients:

- 1 teaspoon coconut oil or ghee
- 1 lb. ground lamb
- 1 medium onion, diced
- 2 teaspoons mild curry powder
- 1 teaspoon ground turmeric
- ¼ teaspoon cayenne powder
- 1/8 teaspoon salt
- 2 sweet potatoes, cubed
- 2 cups chicken broth or water
- ¾ cup canned coconut milk
- 1 teaspoon apple cider vinegar or lemon/lime juice
- 16 oz. kale or spinach
- 16 oz. cauliflower rice

Method:

1. Place a pan over a medium heat and add some oil.
2. Add the onions and cook for five minutes until soft.
3. Add the lamb and cook until browned, stirring often.
4. Add the spices, sweet potatoes and broth and stir again.
5. Cover and bring to a boil then reduce the heat to a simmer and cook for 10 minutes until the potatoes are soft.
6. Stir through the coconut milk, vinegar, greens and cauliflower rice.
7. Serve and enjoy.

Greek Lamb Meatballs

There's something about Greek food that never fails to astonish me. Maybe it's their use of oregano. Perhaps it's their classic take on Mediterranean food. Or could it even be the fact that they know how to make a delicious meat even better? Try these meatballs and you'll see what I mean.

Serves: 4

Time: 35 mins

- Calories: 476
- Net carbs: 17g
- Protein: 22g
- Fat: 35g

Ingredient:

- 1 lb. ground lamb
- Oil, to taste
- 1 free-range egg, beaten
- 1/2 medium onion, finely chopped
- 1 garlic clove, finely minced
- 1/4 cup cassava flour or almond flour
- 2 tablespoons chopped mint
- 2 tablespoons chopped cilantro
- 1 tablespoon cumin powder
- 1 tablespoon sumac powder
- 1 teaspoon salt
- 1 teaspoon ground black pepper

Method:

1. Preheat the oven to 375°F and grease a baking sheet with oil.
2. Take a medium bowl and add all the ingredients.
3. Stir well using your hands then form into the meatball shapes.
4. Place onto the baking sheet then pop into the oven.
5. Cook for 20 minutes until cooked.
6. Serve and enjoy.

Lamb Vindaloo

OK, so if you don't like spicy food you should probably run a mile right now. But if you do, stick around and I'll show you how to make a vindaloo which hits all the right spots and keeps you coming back for more. You have been warned!

Serves: 6

Time: 45 mins

- Calories: 361
- Net carbs: 29g
- Protein: 27g
- Fat: 6g

Ingredients:

For the spice mixture...

- 1 tablespoon ground cumin
- 1 tablespoon ground coriander
- 1 tablespoon ground turmeric
- 1 tablespoon curry powder
- 1/4 teaspoon ground cloves
- 1/4 teaspoon ground cardamom

For the curry...

- 1/8 teaspoon cayenne pepper
- 1 bay leaf
- 1 green bell pepper, diced small
- 1 yellow onion, diced small
- 2 1/2 lb. boneless leg of lamb, cut into bite sized cubes
- Salt and pepper, to taste
- 2 tablespoons ghee
- 2 cloves garlic, finely chopped
- 2 tablespoon tomato paste
- 1/2 cup full fat, unsweetened coconut milk, blended
- 1/2 cup beef broth
- 2 tablespoons vinegar
- 1 teaspoon freshly grated ginger

To serve...

- Cilantro

Method:

1. Place a skillet over a medium heat and add the ghee.
2. Add the meat and cook until browned, then drain off the excess fat and pop to one side.
3. Add the onions and peppers to the pan and cook for five minutes until soft.
4. Add the salt and pepper, garlic and tomato paste and cook for a further minute or two.
5. Add the spice mixture and cook for another minute.
6. Finally throw in the coconut milk, broth and vinegar and stir well.
7. Add the meat back to the pan, add the bay leaf and ginger and stir again.
8. Cover with the lid then simmer for 30 minutes.
9. Serve and enjoy.

Instant Pot Moroccan Lamb Stew

Combining sweet and savory, vegetable and meat and flavors with yet more flavors, this easy Instant Pot stew is great for gatherings, winters nights and days when you need comfort in your belly. It also keeps well so make a big batch and pop it in your fridge.

Serves: 4-6

Time: 45 mins

- Calories: 610
- Net carbs: 50g
- Protein: 36g
- Fat: 29g

Ingredients:

- 1 lb. lamb stew meat, chopped
- 2 cups chopped carrots
- 2 cups chopped sweet potatoes
- 1 medium white onion, chopped
- 3 cups finely chopped kale, stems removed
- 2-3 cloves garlic, chopped
- 4 dried unsweetened apricots, finely chopped
- 2 x 14.5 oz. cans diced tomatoes
- 2.5 cups chicken broth or chicken stock
- 3 tablespoons coconut aminos
- Olive oil
- Salt and pepper, to taste
- 1/2 teaspoon ground ginger
- 1 teaspoon ground cumin
- 1 teaspoon cinnamon
- 1/4 teaspoon curry powder
- 1/4 teaspoon ground turmeric
- 1/4 teaspoon allspice

Method:

1. Open the lid of the Instant Pot, add some olive oil and turn onto sauté mode.
2. Add the meat and cook until browned.
3. Throw in the remaining ingredients, stir well and cover with the lid.
4. Cook for 20 minutes.
5. Do a quick pressure release then open the lid.
6. Use an immersion blender to whizz a small amount of the liquid to thicken the sauce if you wish.
7. Serve and enjoy.

Lamb Tacos

Yes, you can still eat tacos when you're following a wholefood diet and yes, they will taste amazing. Try these easy thyme-flecked tacos and you'll see.

Serves: 4-6

Time: 3 hours

- Calories: 573
- Net carbs: 6g
- Protein: 57g
- Fat: 26g

Ingredients:

For the lamb tacos...

- 2 lb. lamb stew meat or lamb shoulder, cut into 1-inch chunks
- 3 cups chicken stock
- 1 bunch thyme
- 2 tablespoons avocado oil or ghee
- Salt, to taste

For the cauliflower tortillas...

- 1 head cauliflower, broken into florets
- 2 free-range eggs
- Pinch of salt
- Avocado oil

To serve...

- Radishes, sliced thinly
- Chopped cilantro

Method:

1. Place a skillet over a medium heat and add the avocado oil.
2. Place the lamb on a flat surface then sprinkle with salt.
3. Pop into the pan and cook for a few minutes each side.
4. Add the stock and thyme and bring to the boil.
5. Cover with the lid then turn down the heat and cook for 2 hours until tender.
6. Meanwhile, preheat the oven to 375°F and grease and line a baking sheet.
7. Find a food processor, add the cauliflower and whizz until it forms breadcrumbs.
8. Place the cauliflower onto the sheet and pop into the oven for 10 minutes until cooked through.
9. Remove from the oven and allow to cool slightly.
10. Place a clean tea towel over a colander and add the cauliflower. Wrap up and squeeze out any excess moisture, then place into a bowl.

11. Add the eggs and salt and stir well to combine.
12. Take ¼ of the dough and spread into a circle on the baking sheet. Repeat with the remaining ingredients.
13. Pop into the oven and bake for 25 minutes, flipping as needed.
14. When the lamb has cooked, shred with two forks and serve with the tortillas.
15. Enjoy!

Crockpot Greek Lamb Roast

This lamb roast is thick, heavy and filling, just like grandma used to make. It's also totally worth the time it takes to slowly cook it in your crockpot so you can watch the meat just fall off the bone.

Serves: 4

Time: 10 hours

- Calories: 645
- Net carbs: 5g
- Protein: 41g
- Fat: 38g

Ingredients:

- 3 cloves garlic, minced
- 1 small onion, chopped
- 1 lemon, juiced
- 1 tablespoon olive oil
- 2 lb. leg of lamb
- 1/4 teaspoon sea salt
- 1/4 teaspoon ground black pepper
- 1 teaspoon paprika
- 1 teaspoon garlic powder
- 1 teaspoon dried oregano
- 3 sprigs fresh thyme
- 1 sprigs rosemary
- 1 bay leaves
- 1/2 cup chicken stock

Method:

1. Place a skillet over a medium heat and add the oil.
2. Pop the onions into the pan and cook for five minutes until soft.
3. Add the garlic and stir well.
4. Place the lamb into the pan and sear on all sides then transfer to your crockpot.
5. Add the remaining ingredients, cover with the lid then cook on low for 8-10 hours until cooked through.
6. Serve and enjoy.

Instant Pot North African Spiced Lamb Shanks

These incredible lamb shanks ask you to find a magical spice blend called ras el hanout. If you can't get hold of any where you live, just make your own cheat version using equal parts paprika, coriander, ginger and a pinch of saffron.

Serves: 3

Time: 2 hours

- Calories: 522
- Net carbs: 37g
- Protein: 44g
- Fat: 25g

Ingredients:

- 3 lamb shanks
- 2 medium yellow onions, cut into quarters
- 4 large carrots, cut into 2" pieces
- 2 stalks celery, cut into 2" pieces
- 1 bulb fennel, cut into wedges
- 5-6 cloves garlic, smashed peeled and left whole
- 1 cup 100% pomegranate juice
- 1 ½ cups chicken or beef stock
- Salt and pepper, to taste
- *Ras el hanout* spice mix
- Cayenne pepper (opt.)
- 1 tablespoon avocado oil

To serve...

- Toasted slivered almonds

Method:

1. Place the lamb onto a flat surface and season well with *ras el hanout*, salt, pepper and cayenne.
2. Open the Instant Pot, add a tablespoon of the avocado oil and turn onto sauté mode.
3. Add the lamb and brown on all sides. Transfer the meat to a tray and pop to one side.
4. Add the pomegranate juice into the pan and use a wooden spoon to scrape off any browned bits.
5. Pace the lamb back into the pot, cover with the remaining ingredients and bring to the boil.
6. Cover with the lid and cook on manual high for 75 mins.

7. Do a quick pressure release then transfer the lamb and veggies to a tray.
8. Turn the Instant Pot back onto sauté and reduce the sauce down until looking delicious.
9. Serve and enjoy.

Turmeric Garlic Pan Fried Lamb Chops

Garlicky, lemony and flecked with oregano- that just how I like my lamb chops. Yum!

Serves: 4

Time: 30 mins

- Calories: 518
- Net carbs: 11g
- Protein: 34g
- Fat: 36g

Ingredients:

- 1 1/2 lb. lamb rib chops
- 1 tablespoon coconut oil

For the paste...

- 1 tablespoon extra-virgin olive oil
- 1 tablespoon lemon juice
- Zest of 1 lemon
- 4 garlic cloves, minced
- 1 1/2 teaspoons sea salt
- 1/2 teaspoon turmeric powder
- 1/2 teaspoon dried oregano

Method:

1. Grab a medium bowl and add the paste ingredients. Stir well.
2. Place the lamb onto a flat surface and rub into the lamb.
3. Cover and pop into the fridge for at least 30 minutes, preferably overnight.
4. Grab a skillet, add the coconut oil and pop over a medium heat.
5. Cook the lamb for 5-10 minutes on each side until tender then serve and enjoy.

Greek Lamb Kabobs

All you need for these amazing kabobs is a tender cut of lamb, red onion and a handful of Greek flavors and you'll have a meal you'll never forget. Is it authentic? Who knows? But it sure does taste good. (Remember to soak your wooden skewers before using).

Serves: 8

Time: 30 mins

- Calories: 89
- Net carbs: 2g
- Protein: 9g
- Fat: 2g

Ingredients:

- 2 lb. leg lamb, deboned and cubed
- 2 teaspoons salt
- ½ red onion, very roughly chopped

For the marinade...

- 1/3 cup extra virgin olive oil
- Juice of one lemon
- 1–2 tablespoons chopped fresh oregano
- 1 tablespoon fresh thyme
- 3 cloves garlic, finely minced
- ½ teaspoon fresh ground pepper

Method:

1. Find a medium bowl and add the marinade ingredients. Stir well to combine.
2. Add the lamb cubes and the red onion then stir again.
3. Cover and leave in the fridge for 30 minutes, preferably overnight.
4. Preheat your broiler on high then skewer the meat, alternating with red onion pieces.
5. Salt well then cook on high for 10 minutes, turning often.
6. Serve and enjoy.

Main Meals (Fish & Seafood)

Shrimp Scampi with Zucchini Noodles

WOW! So much flavor, so wonderfully gluten-free and so delicious, these shrimps will hit that seafood spot and keep your taste buds happy, I promise.

Serves: 4
Time: 30 mins

- Calories: 255
- Net carbs: 5g
- Protein: 26g
- Fat: 13g

Ingredients:

- 1 lb. shrimp
- 1/4 cup ghee
- 1/3 cup chicken bone broth
- 4-6 cloves garlic, minced
- Pinch red pepper flakes, to taste
- Salt and pepper, to taste
- 1/3 cup parsley, minced
- 1 1/2 tablespoons lemon juice
- 4 medium zucchinis, spiralized and sweat
- 1/2 teaspoon sea salt (for sweating zucchini)
- Olive oil

Method:

1. Grab a large skillet, place over a medium heat and add the butter.
2. Add the garlic and cook for around a minute, being careful not to burn it.
3. Add the broth, salt, red pepper flakes and black pepper and bring to the simmer.
4. Cook for a minute or so until the broth reduces down by about a half then throw in the shrimp.
5. Cook for around five minutes until opaque then remove from the heat.
6. Take a bowl and add the zucchini, lemon juice and parsley and stir through to combine.
7. Place a skillet over a medium heat, add the olive oil then add the noodles.
8. Sautee for a few minutes until tender.
9. Add to the shrimp then serve and enjoy.

Strawberry Cod Ceviche

Strawberries, cucumber, citrus and wild cod come together in this light and nourishing dish that is bound to impress.

Serves: 2

Time: 5 mins (plus 2 hours resting time)

- Calories: 526
- Net carbs: 20g
- Protein: 48g
- Fat: 27g

Ingredients:

- 1/2 cucumber, peeled, deseeded and diced into 1/2-inch cubes
- 1/4 cup cilantro
- 1/2 cup strawberries, diced
- 1/2 pound wild-caught cod, diced
- 5 limes, juiced
- 1/2 avocado, diced
- 1/4 tablespoon sea salt
- 1 tablespoon olive oil

Method:

1. Find a shallow dish, add the cod and pour the lime juice over the top.
2. Cover and pop into the fridge for two hours.
3. Remove from the fridge, pour away the lime juice and add the remaining ingredients.
4. Serve and enjoy.

Purple Sweet Potato Salmon Sushi Rolls

If you're in the mood for something a little different, make sure you create these gorgeously colored sushi rolls. Simple, healthy and bright, they do take some practice to make well. But stick with it- you'll soon master the art of sushi.

Serves: 2

Time: 30 mins

- Calories: 391
- Net carbs: 32g
- Protein: 20g
- Fat: 15g

Ingredients:

- 2 medium sized purple sweet potatoes
- 1 red bell pepper, sliced thinly
- 1 yellow bell pepper, sliced thinly
- 4 oz. wild-caught, sashimi-grade salmon, cut into thin slices
- 1 avocado, sliced thinly
- 1 cucumber, julienned
- 2 Nori sheets
- Olive oil

Method:

1. Place the sweet potato onto a flat surface, prick with a fork and place into the microwave for around 4 minutes until cooked through.
2. Remove from the microwave and allow to cool before peeling off the skin.
3. Mash the potato and pop to one side.
4. Place a nori sheet onto a sushi mat and spread the sweet potato over the entire surface.
5. Top with the salmon and veggies and wrap up tightly.
6. Place the roll onto chopping board then use an extra-sharp knife to slice into pieces.
7. Drizzle with olive oil then serve and enjoy.

Coconut Shrimp with Cilantro Lime Dip

Coated in a healthy and light coconut batter, deliciously crunchy and absolutely perfect when served with the dip, these are well worth the wait. They're also great for a party or gathering and make an excellent healthy (and unexpected) snack.

Serves: 2-4

Time: 45 mins

- Calories: 599
- Net carbs: 7g
- Protein: 34g
- Fat: 43g

Ingredients:

For the coconut shrimp...

- 8 medium raw, wild-caught shrimp
- 1 free-range egg, beaten
- 3 tablespoons unsweetened shredded coconut
- 1/2 tablespoon coconut flour
- 1 tablespoon avocado oil

For the cilantro lime dip...

- 1/4 cup raw cashews, soaked in warm water for 4 hours
- 2 tablespoons chopped cilantro
- 1 teaspoon lime juice
- 1 garlic clove, minced
- 1/2 teaspoon salt
- 1/8 teaspoon fresh-ground black pepper
- 2 tablespoons filtered water

Method:

1. Preheat the oven to 300°F and line a baking sheet with parchment paper.
2. Take a medium bowl and add the shredded coconut and coconut flour. Stir to combine.
3. Take another bowl and add the egg, beating well
4. Dip the shrimp into the egg, allowing any excess to drip off.
5. Next place into the coconut mixture then place onto the pan.
6. Repeat with the remaining shrimp then pop into the oven.
7. Cook for 20 minutes until brown then flip and bake for another 20 minutes.
8. Meanwhile, drain the water from the cashews and place into a food processor. Add the remaining ingredients then whizz until creamy and smooth.
9. Serve and enjoy.

Fish Taco Bowls with Spicy Mayo

Love fish tacos? I've got your back. Throw together these ingredients and you'll discover that you can cook better than any takeout. Don't believe me? Try these!

Serves: 2

Time: 15 mins

- Calories: 399
- Net carbs: 24g
- Protein: 28g
- Fat: 22g

Ingredients:

- 2 cups riced cauliflower
- 4 cups shredded cabbage
- 2 x 4 oz. filets mahi mahi
- 1 tablespoon taco seasoning
- 1/2 tablespoon + 1 teaspoon avocado oil
- 1 tablespoon lime juice
- 1/4 cup cilantro, roughly chopped
- 1/2 cup mango salsa (no added sugar)
- 1/2 large avocado

For the pickled onions...

- 1/2 cup red onion, thinly sliced
- 1/2 cup apple cider vinegar
- Water, as needed
- 1 teaspoon salt

For the mayo...

- 2 tablespoons mayo (recipe available in this book)
- Chipotle sauce, to taste

To serve...

- Jalapeños
- Cilantro
- Lime wedges

Method:

1. Find a jar and add the onions, vinegar, water and salt. Cover with the lid, shake well then pop to one side.
2. Place a large skillet over a medium heat and add a tablespoon of oil.
3. Add the coconut rice and cook for five minutes.
4. Add the lime and cilantro, stir well then pop to one side.

121

5. Place the fish into a shallow dish, coat with the taco seasoning and rub into the flesh.
6. Find another pan, place over a medium heat and add the remaining oil.
7. Add the fish and cook for 3-5 minutes on each side until cooked.
8. Find two bowls and add the cabbage, cauliflower rice, salsa and avocado.
9. Find a small bowl and add the mayo and chipotle sauce. Stir well together then add to the bowls.
10. Top with the fish and any extra toppings.
11. Serve and enjoy.

Crispy Salmon Cakes

Could cooking get any faster? Simply combine in a bowl and fry for a fast, tummy-pleasing treat that takes good care of your health.

Serves: 5

Time: 15 mins

- Calories: 223
- Net carbs: 2g
- Protein: 17g
- Fat: 16g

Ingredients:

- 2 x 12 oz. cans wild caught salmon
- 3 sprigs fresh cilantro, minced
- 3 sprigs fresh oregano, minced
- 3 cloves garlic, minced
- 1 lemon, zested and juiced
- 1 teaspoon ground cumin
- 1 teaspoon black pepper
- 1 teaspoon onion powder
- ½ teaspoon fine salt
- 1 tablespoon olive oil
- 2 large free-range eggs
- 3 tablespoons flax meal
- 2 tablespoons olive oil

Method:

1. Place a skillet over a medium heat.
2. Take a large bowl and add the salmon, herbs, lemon zest and juice, cumin, pepper, onion, salt and 1 tablespoon of olive oil. Stir well.
3. Add the eggs and the flax meal then stir again.
4. Shape into six patties then pop to one side for a second.
5. Add the remaining oil to the skillet.
6. When the oil is hot, add the patties and cook for 4-5 minutes each side until brown.
7. Remove from the heat and place onto paper towels.
8. Serve and enjoy.

Tandoori Tuna and Cauliflower Rice Bake

This delicious dish is sure to please the whole family, keep them filled and ensure that they're getting everything they need to stay healthy and junk-food free.

Serves: 4

Time: 45 mins

- Calories: 459
- Net carbs: 13g
- Protein: 17g
- Fat: 28g

Ingredients:

- ½ cup mayonnaise (see recipe here)
- 3/4 cup full fat coconut milk, blended
- 2 tablespoons cashew butter
- 1 teaspoon arrowroot powder
- 1 teaspoon garlic powder
- 1 teaspoon ground ginger
- ½ teaspoon ground cumin
- ½ teaspoon cinnamon
- 1 teaspoon salt
- ¼ teaspoon black pepper
- 4 cups raw cauliflower rice
- 2 bell peppers, sliced
- 3 cans tuna
- Juice of 1 lime

Method:

1. Preheat the oven to 400°F and grease a 9 x 13" casserole dish.
2. Take a large bowl and add the mayo, coconut milk, cashew butter, arrowroot and the spices. Whisk until combined.
3. Add the cauliflower rice, peppers, tuna and lime juice. Stir again to combine.
4. Pop into the casserole dish and spread out.
5. Pop into the oven for 30 minutes until the cauliflower is cooked through then serve and enjoy.

Spiced Mexican Tuna Steak with Avocado Salsa

Everyone loves Mexican-style tuna, don't they? If not, you're going to go crazy when you try this amazing dish. Feel free to pimp with extra chili or veggies if you're a fan of spice.

Serves: 2

Time: 35 mins

- Calories: 393
- Net carbs: 12g
- Protein: 9g
- Fat: 32g

Ingredients:

- 3 tablespoons coconut oil
- 1 medium red onion, sliced
- 1 medium red pepper, sliced
- 2/3 teaspoon sweet paprika
- 2/3 teaspoon cumin powder
- Pinch of red chili flakes
- 1 large garlic clove, diced finely
- 1 tablespoon apple cider vinegar
- 1 tablespoon olive oil or coconut oil
- 1 tablespoon ghee
- 1 teaspoon coriander seeds
- 2 tuna steaks
- 1 lime
- Pinch sea salt & black pepper
- 1 large ripe avocado, chopped
- 2 tablespoons cilantro, chopped
- Juice of ½ lime
- A little pinch of sea salt

Method:

1. Place the tuna onto a flat surface and sprinkle with salt and pepper. Drizzle with olive oil.
2. Pop a skillet over a medium heat and add the coconut oil.
3. Add the onions and peppers and cook for five minutes until soft.
4. Add the paprika, cumin, chili, garlic, vinegar, salt and two tablespoons of water.
5. Mix well and cook for another few minutes then turn off the heat and pop to one side.
6. Find another skillet, pop over a medium heat and add the ghee.

7. Add the coriander seeds and zest of a lime and cook for 30 seconds.
8. Add the tuna steaks, drizzle with juice from half a lime and cook for 2 minutes on each side.
9. Use a spoon and bathe the tuna in the ghee and spice cooking mixture then remove from the heat.
10. Find a small bowl, add the avocado and coriander and season with salt and remaining lime juice.
11. Place the red peppers on the places, add the tuna, top with the avocado salsa, add more peppers if required then serve and enjoy.

Braised Salmon in Creamy Mushroom Sauce

Give traditional creamy mushroom sauce a facelift by tweaking it with coconut milk and cayenne for a tasty, surprising meal. This dish also works brilliantly with fresh herbs so do throw some in if you have some to hand.

Serves: 4

Time: 30 mins

- Calories: 459
- Net carbs: 14g
- Protein: 32g
- Fat: 30g

Ingredients:

- 4 tablespoons + 1 tablespoon ghee, divided
- 4 salmon fillets, skin removed
- Salt and pepper, to taste
- Paprika, to taste
- 1 onion, sliced
- 2 garlic cloves, finely minced
- 1 red jalapeno pepper, diced
- 3.5 oz. shitake mushrooms, sliced
- 1 tablespoon coconut aminos
- 1 cup coconut milk
- 1/4 cup seafood stock
- 1 cup baby spinach leaves
- 1 teaspoon cayenne pepper

Method:

1. Place a skillet over a medium heat and add the 2 tablespoons of ghee.
2. Pop the salmon onto a flat surface and add the salt, pepper and paprika.
3. Sear the salmon for about 3 minutes on each side then remove from the pan and pop to one side.
4. Add another 2 tablespoons of the ghee then cook the onions for five minutes until soft.
5. Throw in the garlic and jalapeno peppers and cook for another minute.
6. Season with salt and pepper then add the mushrooms and coconut aminos.
7. Stir in the teaspoon of ghee and cook until the mushrooms are tender, stirring often.
8. Add the broth, coconut milk, spinach and cayenne and stir well.

9. Return the salmon to the pot and cook for 5 minutes or so until the sauce starts to thicken.
10. Turn on your broiler and pop the skillet into the oven.
11. Broil for five minutes until browned.
12. Serve and enjoy.

Easy Paleo Pecan-crusted Salmon

Pecans make a delicious crust to this omega-3 rich salmon dish. As you tuck into each tender bite, you'll know that you're giving your brain, heart and taste buds exactly what they need to thrive.

Serves: 3

Time: 40 mins

- Calories: 247
- Net carbs: 10g
- Protein: 43g
- Fat: 32g

Ingredients:

- 1 cup pecans or walnuts
- 3/4 teaspoon salt
- 1/2 teaspoon freshly ground black pepper
- 2 teaspoons Italian seasoning
- 1/8 teaspoon smoked paprika
- 3 1/2 tablespoons coconut oil
- 2 x 8 oz. salmon fillets
- Lemon slices (opt.)

Method:

1. Preheat your oven to 350°F and lightly grease a casserole dish.
2. Pop the pecans into the casserole dish, put into the oven and cook for 5-10 minutes until toasted, stirring often.
3. Remove the pecans from the oven then turn the heat up to 400°F. Whiz until smooth.
4. Grab your blender and add the pecans, salt, pepper, herbs, paprika and coconut oil.
5. Place the salmon into the casserole dish, top with the pecan mixture and pop into the oven.
6. Bake for 15-20 minutes until brown then serve and enjoy.

Seafood Stir Fry

If you're feeling like a fast and tasty meal, roll up your sleeves and get cooking this amazing Cajun meal. Rich, satisfying and nourishing, it's the perfect comfort food whenever you need a treat.

Serves: 4

Time: 30 mins

- Calories: 277
- Net carbs: 9g
- Protein: 58g
- Fat: 9g

Ingredients:

- 2 tablespoons ghee
- 1 lb. shrimp, peeled and deveined
- 1 lb. white fish, cut into bite-sized cubed
- 1 onion, sliced into thin strips
- 4 cups broccoli florets
- 6 ribs celery, thinly sliced
- 4 cloves garlic, minced
- 2 tablespoons clam juice
- 1 tablespoons coconut aminos
- 1 teaspoon arrowroot starch

For the Cajun seasoning…

- 1 teaspoon sea salt
- 1 teaspoon garlic powder
- 1 teaspoon smoked paprika
- 1 teaspoon dried thyme
- 1/2 teaspoon oregano
- 1/2 teaspoon onion powder
- 1/4 teaspoon ground pepper
- 1/4 teaspoon cayenne

To serve…

- Green onions, sliced
- Pinch red pepper flakes

Method:

1. Find a medium bowl and add the Cajun seasoning ingredients. Stir well.
2. Take another bowl and add the clam juice, aminos, seasoning and arrowroot. Stir and pop to one side.

3. Place a skillet over a medium heat and add the ghee.
4. Add the shrimp and fish to the pan and cook for 5 minutes, stirring often.
5. Remove from a pan and place onto a plate.
6. Pop the onion, broccoli and celery into the skillet and cook for five minutes until the veggies soften.
7. Add the garlic and cook for an extra minute.
8. Pour in the sauce and stir well to combine, then add the seafood back into the pot.
9. Stir through then serve and enjoy.

Main Meals (Vegetarian & Vegan)

Zucchini Pasta

Craving tomato pasta and don't have much time to cook. Try this. You can thank me later.

Serves: 4
Time: 20 mins

- Calories: 236
- Net carbs: 15g
- Protein: 9g
- Fat: 16g

Ingredients:

- 2 lb. zucchini, spiralized
- 2 cups diced tomatoes
- 1 large red onion, thinly sliced
- 4 garlic cloves, minced
- 1/4 cup extra virgin olive oil
- 1/2 cup fresh basil
- Salt and pepper, to taste
- 1/2 teaspoon crushed red pepper (opt.)

Method:

1. Place a skillet over a medium heat and add the olive oil.
2. Add the onion and cook for five minutes until soft.
3. Throw in the garlic and cook for a further minute.
4. Add the zucchini noodles, season well then cook for another 2 minutes.
5. Add the tomatoes and cook for another few minutes.
6. Finally, throw in the basil, red pepper and parmesan then stir well.
7. Serve and enjoy.

Creamy Spinach Sweet Potato Noodles with Cashew Sauce

Sweet potato noodles make a surprising and satisfying alternative to regular noodles and they work perfectly with the creamy, nutty cashew sauce. Add whatever veggie your heart desires and you can create an awesome meal that will keep you satisfied for hours.

Serves: 4-6

Time: 25 mins

- Calories: 187
- Net carbs: 8g
- Protein: 4g
- Fat: 16g

Ingredients:

- 1 cup cashews
- 3/4 cup water (plus more for soaking)
- 1/2 teaspoon salt
- 1 clove garlic
- 1 tablespoon oil
- 4 large sweet potatoes, spiralized
- 2 cups baby spinach
- A handful of fresh basil leaves, chives, or other herbs
- Salt and pepper, to taste
- Olive oil

Method:

1. Place the cashews into a bowl, cover with water and soak for two hours.
2. Drain the cashews then place into a food processor.
3. Add the water, salt and garlic then hit whizz and puree until smooth. Set to one side.
4. Place a skillet over a medium heat, add the oil then add the sweet potatoes.
5. Cook for 5-10 minutes until tender then remove from the heat and add the spinach. Stir through.
6. Add half of the herbs and half of the sauce and toss again.
7. Add salt, pepper, olive oil and the remaining herbs.
8. Serve and enjoy.

Vegetarian Power Bowls

The concept behind this dish is simple- roast your favorite veggies, top with a creamy, dreamy sauce and throw hard-boiled eggs and whatever else you fancy onto the top. Amazing!

Serves: 4
Time: 50 mins

- Calories: 361
- Net carbs: 27g
- Protein: 16g
- Fat: 19g

Ingredients:

- 2 tablespoons extra-virgin olive oil, divided
- 1 small red onion, cut into 1-inch wedges
- 2 large sweet potatoes, skins on and halved lengthwise
- 2 teaspoons chili powder, divided
- 3/4 teaspoon salt, divided
- 3/4 teaspoon black pepper, divided
- 1 small head broccoli or cauliflower
- 1 small bunch kale, large stems removed

For the dressing...

- Juice of 1 lemon
- 3 tablespoons tahini or almond butter
- 1 clove garlic, minced
- 1/2-1 teaspoon ground cumin
- 1/4 teaspoon salt

To serve...

- 4 hard-boiled eggs

Method:

1. Preheat your oven to 400°F and grease a baking sheet.
2. Place the sweet potatoes and onions onto the baking sheet.
3. Drizzle with the olive and sprinkle with the chili, salt and pepper. Stir well to combine.
4. Pop into the oven and bake for 10 minutes.
5. Add the broccoli or cauliflower to the pan, stir well then return to the oven.
6. Cook for 20 more minutes until the veggies are tender.
7. Remove from the oven, add the kale, drizzle with extra oil and seasonings if required, stir well then op back into the oven for five more minutes.

8. Grab a small bowl and add the dressing ingredients. Add hot water as required to make the sauce to your required consistency.
9. Serve with the hardboiled eggs and enjoy.

Vegan Creamy Curry

Although there might appear to be a ton of ingredients, this curry is perfectly simple and utterly delicious. If you don't have the veggies on this list in your fridge, don't worry. Just throw in whatever you have (adjusting cooking times where needed) and you'll be utterly spoiled.

Serves: 6

Time: 40 mins

- Calories: 329
- Net carbs: 11g
- Protein: 5g
- Fat: 29g

Ingredient:

- 1 bell pepper, diced
- 12 oz. cauliflower florets
- 10 oz. broccoli florets
- 10 oz. eggplant, cubed
- 6 tablespoons olive oil
- 1 teaspoon coarse salt
- ¼ teaspoon ground black pepper

For the sauce...

- 2 tablespoons chopped garlic
- 1 tablespoon chopped ginger
- 2 large shallots, finely chopped
- 1 teaspoon turmeric
- 1 teaspoon coriander
- 1 teaspoon ground cumin
- 14 oz. full fat coconut milk, blended
- 1 1/2 tablespoons almond butter or sunbutter
- 1 tablespoon lime juice

Method:

1. Preheat the oven to 420°F and grease a baking sheet.
2. Place the veggies onto the baking sheet, season with olive oil, salt and pepper and stir well to combine.
3. Pop into the oven and bake for 25-30 minutes.
4. After 15 minutes cooking time has elapsed, place a skillet over a medium heat.
5. Add the onion and cook for five minutes then throw in the garlic and cook for a further minute.

6. Turn down the heat then add the spices and cook for 30 seconds.
7. Stir in coconut milk, almond butter and lime juice.
8. When the veggies are cooked, remove from the oven and combine with the curry sauce.
9. Serve and enjoy.

Mushroom Risotto with Cauliflower Rice

Creamy, scrumptious and packed full of veggie goodness, this is a risotto that you'll find yourself making time and time again. I love to play with the flavors with this one, so feel free to add herbs, spices or my all-time favorite- chili!

Serves: 4-6
Time: 30 mins

- Calories: 70
- Net carbs: 8g
- Protein: 5g
- Fat: 3g

Ingredients:

- 1 large head cauliflower, cut into florets
- 1 tablespoon coconut oil
- 1 large yellow onion, diced
- 2 large garlic cloves, minced
- ¾ lb. mushrooms, thinly sliced
- ½ cup vegetable stock
- Fresh parsley, chopped
- Salt and pepper, to taste

Method:

1. Find a food processor and whizz the cauliflower into rice-like pieces, then pop to one side.
2. Place a skillet over a medium heat and add the coconut oil.
3. Add the onions and cook for five minutes until soft.
4. Add the garlic, stir and cook for a further minute.
5. Throw in the mushrooms and cook until soft.
6. Add the cauliflower rice and stock and turn down the heat.
7. Cook for 10 minutes until the cauliflower is soft.
8. Season with salt and pepper, garnish and enjoy!

Meatless Buffalo Burgers

With just 6 ingredient and no sight of tofu or beans, these gut-friendly buffalo burgers are perfect for any occasion, whether you're having veggie-friendly BBQ or just chilling with your buddies. Enjoy!

Serves: 8

Time: 45 mins

- Calories: 125
- Net carbs: 10g
- Protein: 6g
- Fat: 7g

Ingredients:

- 4 cups riced cauliflower
- 1/2 cup cooked, mashed sweet potato
- 2 free-range eggs
- 3 tablespoons buffalo sauce
- 1/2 cup finely diced yellow onion
- 1 cup + 2 tablespoons almond flour
- 1/2 teaspoon salt

Method:

1. Preheat your oven to 375°C and line a baking sheet with parchment paper.
2. Take a large bowl and add the cauliflower, mashed potatoes, eggs, buffalo sauce, onion, almond flour and salt.
3. Stir well to combine.
4. Form into patties using your hands then place onto the parchment paper.
5. Pop into the oven and bake for 35 mins until cooked through.
6. Serve and enjoy.

"Cheesy" Broccoli Casserole

Broccoli and cheese are like a match made in heaven and they can be a healthy match when you create this easy, delicious casserole. Creamy, tasty and filling, what more could you need for your vegetarian meal?

Serves: 12

Time: 1 hour 15 mins

- Calories: 176
- Net carbs: 11g
- Protein: 6g
- Fat: 13g

Ingredients:

- 2 lb. broccoli florets
- 1 tablespoons coconut oil
- 1 onion, chopped
- 4 garlic cloves, minced

For the 'cheese' sauce...

- 1 1/2 cup full-fat coconut milk, blended
- 1 cup raw cashews
- 3/4 cup nutritional yeast
- 1/3 cup apple cider vinegar
- 2 tablespoons Dijon mustard
- 1 teaspoon onion powder
- 2 teaspoon sea salt
- 1/2 teaspoon ground black pepper
- 1/2 teaspoon smoked paprika
- 2 free-range eggs

To serve...

- Fresh parsley

Method:

1. Preheat the oven to 350°F and grease a 9 x 13" baking dish.
2. Place the broccoli into the bottom.
3. Pop a skillet over a medium heat, add the coconut oil and throw in the onion.
4. Cook for five minutes until soft then throw in the garlic and cook for a further minute.
5. Remove from the heat and place into the baking dish with the broccoli.
6. Grab your blender and add the 'cheese' sauce ingredients, except the eggs. Whizz until smooth.

7. Add the eggs and pulse until mixed through.
8. Pour over the broccoli then pop into the oven.
9. Bake for an hour then serve and enjoy.

Caramelized Leek, Fennel & Onion Gratin

Mmmm...my mouth is watering just thinking about his fragrant and tasty dish. 100% vegan, gluten-free, grain free and dairy-free, it's healthy yet incredible. Serve with a side salad and you have a complete meal that you'll never forget. It also stores brilliantly in the fridge so feel free to include it as part of your meal prep.

Serves: 6
Time: 45 mins
- Calories: 488
- Net carbs: 45g
- Protein: 12g
- Fat: 25g

Ingredients:
- 2 tablespoons olive oil or coconut oil
- 3 leeks, thinly sliced
- 2 white onions, thinly sliced
- 2 small fennel bulbs, thinly sliced
- 2 cloves garlic, crushed
- 1/4 teaspoon salt
- 1/2 cup cashews (soaked in boiling water for 10 minutes)
- 3/4 cup almond milk
- 1 tablespoons Dijon mustard
- 1/2 teaspoon pepper
- 2 tablespoons nutritional yeast
- 1 cup vegetable or chicken stock
- 1 teaspoon fresh thyme

Method:
1. Preheat the oven to 350°F.
2. Drain the cashews then add to your high-speed blender with the almond milk. Blend until smooth.
3. Pour into a saucepan and add the mustard, pepper, nutritional yeast and stock.
4. Simmer for five minutes until the sauce starts to thicken.
5. Add the thyme then remove from the heat.
6. Place a skillet over a medium heat, add the oil then throw in the leeks, onion, fennel and garlic. Sprinkle with salt then cook for 10 minutes until soft.
7. Pour the cashew cream into the skillet and stir well.
8. Pop the skillet into the oven and bake for 20 minutes until golden.
9. Serve and enjoy.

Baked Eggs with Spring Vegetables

Keep it simple by creating this easy sheet pan meal. Boasting the perfect balance of healthy carbs, proteins and antioxidants, you'll be spoiling your body and definitely filling your plate up again and again. Yum!

Serves: 4

Time: 40 mins

- Calories: 183
- Net carbs: 9g
- Protein: 12g
- Fat: 12g

Ingredients:

- 1 large beet
- 2 red potatoes or 1 sweet potato
- 1 bunch radish, sliced
- Salt and pepper, to taste
- 2 garlic cloves, crushed or minced
- 1–2 tablespoons olive oil
- Lemon
- 1 zucchini
- ½ red onion, sliced
- 1–2 cups leafy greens such as kale or spinach or both
- 6-8 free-range eggs

To serve...

- Nutritional yeast
- Chopped fresh herbs
- Sliced green onion

Method:

1. Preheat your oven to 400°F and grease a baking sheet.
2. Grab a large bowl and add the veggies (except the zucchini and the kale) with the oil, salt, pepper and the juice of half a lemon.
3. Pop into the oven and bake for 15-20 minutes until tender.
4. Remove from the oven and add the zucchini and kale. Stir well.
5. Make 6 small holes into the veggies and crack the eggs inside.
6. Pop back into the oven for 10-15 minutes until the eggs have set then serve and enjoy.

BBQ Jackfruit

Jackfruit is a favorite meat alternative of mine as it's so delicious, works brilliantly with practically any other food and it's easy to make. Serve with this excellent healthy BBQ sauce for a taste that is simply out of this world.

Serves: 8
Time: 30 mins

- Calories: 137
- Net carbs: 28g
- Protein: 1g
- Fat: 2g

Ingredients:

For the BBQ sauce...

- 1/2 cup hot water
- 4 Medjool dates, pits removed
- 1 1/4 cup tomato sauce
- 1 1/2 tablespoons apple cider vinegar
- 1 tablespoon chili powder
- 2 teaspoons paprika
- 2 teaspoon onion powder
- 1 teaspoon garlic powder
- 1 teaspoon cumin
- 1 teaspoon salt
- 1/2 teaspoon mustard powder

For the jackfruit...

- 1 tablespoon avocado oil
- 1 medium onion
- 2 cans young, green jackfruit in brine

Method:

1. Grab a small bowl, add the dates and soak in the hot water for two minutes.
2. Find your blender and add the dates and the water. Whizz until smooth.
3. Place a pan over a medium heat and add the date mixture plus the remaining sauce ingredients.
4. Bring to a simmer and cook for five minutes, stirring often.
5. Remove from the heat and pop to one side.
6. Place a skillet over a medium heat, add the oil then throw in the onion. Cook for five minutes until soft.
7. Add the jackfruit and cook for 5 minutes more.
8. Add the barbeque sauce, stir well then serve and enjoy.

Thai Curry Grilled Veggie Burgers

If you're not a fan of tofu, you'll adore these nutty veggie burgers. Served with whatever salad you fancy, they'll satisfy your cravings and fill you up.

Serves: 4
Time: 40 mins

- Calories: 296
- Net carbs: 14g
- Protein: 9g
- Fat: 22g

Ingredients:

For the burgers...

- 1/2 cup walnuts
- 1 tablespoon olive oil
- 2 cups cauliflower, cut into florets
- 1/4 cup fresh cilantro, chopped
- 2 tablespoons toasted sesame seeds
- 2 tablespoons natural peanut butter
- 2 tablespoons unsweetened applesauce
- 1 tablespoon coconut flour
- 2 teaspoons yellow curry powder
- 1/2 teaspoon salt
- Pinch of black pepper
- 1 1/2 tablespoons green onion, sliced

For the sauce...

- 1/3 cup avocado, mashed,
- ½ large avocado
- 1 tablespoon full-fat coconut milk, blended
- Salt and pepper, to taste

To serve...

- Olive oil
- Lettuce
- Bean sprouts
- Toasted peanuts

Method:

1. Start by preheating your oven to 350°F.
2. Find a small baking pan and place the walnuts inside.
3. Pop into the oven and toast for 10-15 minutes.

4. Take a skillet, place over a medium heat and add the oil.
5. Grab your food processor and add all the burger ingredients except the green onion.
6. Use your hands and form into 4 patties.
7. Pop into the skillet and cook for 6 minutes on each side until cooked.
8. Take a small food processor, add the sauce ingredients and whizz until smooth.
9. Serve and enjoy.

Dressings

Creamy Avocado Cilantro Lime Dressing

Serves: 4
Time: 5 mins

- Calories: 208
- Net carbs: 7g
- Protein: 3g
- Fat: 18g

Ingredients:

- 1 large avocado
- 1 handful cilantro
- 1/4 cup olive oil
- 2-4 tablespoons water thin to taste
- Juice from 1 lemon/lime
- 1 large garlic clove
- 1 teaspoon sea salt

Method:

1. Grab your food processer, add all ingredients and whizz until smooth.
2. Store in the fridge for up to a week.

Easy Homemade Mayo

Serves: 10
Time: 5 mins
- Calories: 150
- Net carbs: 1g
- Protein: 1g
- Fat: 16g

Ingredients:
- 1 large free-range egg
- 2 teaspoons fresh lemon juice
- 2 teaspoons spicy brown mustard
- 1/4 teaspoon salt
- 3/4 cup olive oil

Method:
1. Find a tall jug and add all the ingredients.
2. Using an immersion blender, whizz on high for about 30 seconds until creamy.
3. Store in the fridge.

Ranch Dressing

Serves: 12

Time: 5 mins

- Calories: 188
- Net carbs: 3g
- Protein: 0g
- Fat: 20g

Ingredients:

- 1 tablespoon lemon juice
- 1/2 cup almond milk
- 1 cup garlic mayonnaise (1 cup <u>mayonnaise</u> with 1 clove garlic)
- 1/4 cup fresh parsley, chopped
- Few drops white vinegar
- Freshly cracked black pepper, to taste
- Salt, to taste

Method:

1. Grab a measuring jug and add the almond milk and lemon juice. Stir well and leave to sit until 'curdled'.
2. Take a bowl and add the mayonnaise, parsley and vinegar and stir well. Slowly add the 'buttermilk' and stir well until you reach your desired consistency.
3. Season with salt and pepper then store in the fridge.

Creamy Chicken Spinach Artichoke Dip

This dip is so much more than a dip. It's a secret meal disguised as a dip! But seriously, it's amazing teamed with potatoes, it's packed with protein and I think it's awesome.

Serves: 8

Time: 35 mins

- Calories: 338
- Net carbs: 5g
- Protein: 16g
- Fat: 27g

Ingredients:

- 1 lb. chicken breasts or tenderloins
- 1 tablespoons olive or avocado oil
- Salt and pepper, to taste
- 1 tablespoons ghee or coconut oil
- 1 medium onion, chopped
- 3-4 cloves garlic, finely chopped
- Sea salt, to taste
- 10 oz. fresh baby spinach, chopped
- 14 oz. can artichoke hearts, drained and chopped

For the dressing...

- 2/3 cup coconut cream
- 1/2 cup mayonnaise
- 1 tablespoons lemon juice
- 3 tablespoons nutritional yeast
- 1/2 teaspoon sea salt
- Black pepper, to taste

Method:

1. Preheat your oven to 400°F and grease a baking sheet with olive oil.
2. Place the chicken onto the baking sheet, drizzle with oil and season well.
3. Pop into the oven and bake for 20 minutes until cooked through.
4. Remove from the oven and pop to one side to cool.
5. Meanwhile, place a skillet over a medium heat and add the oil.
6. Cook the onions for five minutes until soft then add the garlic and cook for another minute.
7. Add the spinach, stir through then add the artichokes.
8. Heat through, season then remove from the heat and pop to one side.
9. Find a large bowl and add the dressing ingredients. Stir well until combined.

10. Once the chicken has cooked through, remove from the oven and shred using two forks.
11. Add the chicken to the other ingredients, stir well then pop into a casserole dish.
12. Pop into the oven and cook for 10 minutes until warmed through.
13. Remove from the oven then serve and enjoy.

Spinach and Artichoke Avocado Dip

Serves: 6
Time: 15 mins
- Calories: 187
- Net carbs: 12g
- Protein: 4g
- Fat: 15g

Ingredients:
- 3 ripe avocados
- 1 teaspoon salt
- 1/2 teaspoon black pepper
- 2 tablespoons mayonnaise
- 2 lemons, juiced
- 1 teaspoon apple cider vinegar
- 1 teaspoon crushed red pepper
- 3 cloves garlic, minced
- 1 teaspoon nutritional yeast
- 12 oz. quartered marinated artichoke hearts, drained
- 2 cups baby spinach, packed

Method:
1. Find your food processor and add all the ingredients except the artichokes and spinach.
2. Whizz until smooth and creamy.
3. Remove the lid and add the artichokes and half of the spinach. Whizz until combined then add the remaining spinach. Serve and enjoy.

Buffalo Chicken Dip

Serves: 8
Time: 40 mins

- Calories: 318
- Net carbs: 3g
- Protein: 16g
- Fat: 26g

Ingredients:

- 1 1/4 lb. chicken tenders or boneless skinless breasts
- 1 tablespoons olive oil
- Sea salt and pepper, to taste
- 1/2 medium onion, chopped
- 2 cloves garlic, minced
- 1 tablespoons ghee or olive oil

For the dressing...

- 2/3 cup mayonnaise
- 2/3 cup coconut cream
- 1 tablespoon brown mustard
- 1 teaspoon garlic powder
- 1 teaspoon onion powder
- 1 teaspoon dried dill
- 1/2 teaspoon smoked paprika
- 1/3 cup hot sauce (sugar free)
- 1 1/2 tablespoons fresh lemon juice

Method:

1. Preheat oven to 400°F and grease a baking sheet with oil.
2. Place the chicken onto the baking sheet, drizzle with oil and season well.
3. Pop into the oven cook for 20 mins until cooked through.
4. Remove from the oven and leave to cool. Turn down the oven to 350°F.
5. Place a skillet over a medium heat, add some oil and cook the onions for five minutes until cooked.
6. Throw in the garlic, stir and cook for a further minute. Remove from the heat and pop to one side.
7. Take a large bowl and add the ingredients for the dressing. Stir well the pop to one side.
8. Place the chicken onto a flat surface and use two forks to shred. Add to the dressing ingredients, throw in the onion and garlic mixture and give it all a stir.

9. Pop into a casserole dish and place into the oven for 20 minutes until warmed through.
10. Serve and enjoy.

Tzatziki Sauce

Serves: 6
Time: 5 mins
- Calories: 657
- Net carbs: 91g
- Protein: 16g
- Fat: 28g

Ingredients:
- 1 x 14 oz. can coconut cream
- 1 medium cucumber, peeled and grated
- 2 tablespoons lemon juice
- 1 teaspoon garlic powder
- 1 teaspoon onion powder
- 2-3 tablespoons fresh dill, chopped
- 1/2 teaspoon salt

Method:
1. Grab a large bowl and add all the ingredients. Stir well until combined.
2. Pop into the fridge for at least an hour before serving.
3. Enjoy!

Treats & Desserts

Almond Butter Banana Cookies

These cookies are entirely amazing, deliciously almondy and super easy to make. A fab project for kids, they're high in protein, perfectly sweet yet oh so healthy.

Makes: 24

Time: 25 mins

- Calories: 58
- Net carbs: 7g
- Protein: 2g
- Fat: 3g

Ingredients:

- 2 ripe bananas, mashed
- 1/2 cup almond flour
- 1/2 cup almond butter
- 1/4 cup cocoa powder
- 1/2 cup raisins

Method:

1. Preheat your oven to 350°F and line two baking sheets with paper. Pop to one side.
2. Find a large bowl and add the bananas, almond flour, almond butter and cocoa.
3. Stir until combined then add the raisins.
4. Drop onto the pre-prepared baking sheets to form cookies then pop into the oven.
5. Cook for 10-12 minutes then leave to cool.
6. Serve and enjoy!

Cherry Banana Ice Cream

Who doesn't love a bowl of ice cream on a hot day? Or a rainy day. Or a cold day. Or pretty much any day at all. Feel free to switch the cherries for another fruit of your choice- blackberries, currants and even mango work amazingly well.

Serves: 2

Time: 10 mins

- Calories: 142
- Net carbs:36g
- Protein: 2g
- Fat: 1g

Ingredients:

- 2 ripe, frozen bananas
- 1 cup frozen cherries
- Organic unsweetened coconut flakes
- Raw organic cacao nibs

Method:

1. Grab your blender and add the frozen bananas and frozen cherries.
2. Whiz until creamy.
3. Sprinkle with the coconut and cacao and then serve and enjoy.

Key Lime Pie Bites

These incredible key lime bites will last for about a week in the fridge but I'm pretty sure they won't last longer than about 10 minutes. Just try and you'll see!

Serves: 8

Time: 10 mins

- Calories: 72
- Net carbs: 3g
- Protein: 3g
- Fat: 5g

Ingredients:

- 1/2 cup pecans
- 1 tablespoon hemp seeds
- 5 dates
- 1 tablespoon lime juice
- 1 tablespoon lime zest
- Coconut water
- 1 tablespoon shredded unsweetened coconut

Optional extras...

- Coconut
- Lime zest

Method:

1. Grab your food processor and add the pecans. Whizz until they form a flour.
2. Add the rest of the ingredients and pulse until they form a dough.
3. Use your hands to form into balls.
4. Roll in coconut and lime zest if required then serve and enjoy.

Nutty Seedy Cacao Bites

When you're looking for a high-protein and chocolately treat, try these ones. They're fast, tasty and make the perfect guilt-free comfort food.

Serves: 12
Time: 10 mins

- Calories: 351
- Net carbs: 22g
- Protein: 10g
- Fat: 25g

Ingredients:

- 1/2 cup cashews
- 1 cup almonds
- 1 cup pitted dates
- ¼ cup hemp hearts
- 2 tablespoons chia seeds
- ½ cup cashew butter
- ¼ cup cacao nibs
- 3 tablespoons water
- Pinch salt

Method:

1. Grab your food processor and add the cashews and almonds. Whizz until the nuts have ground down into chunks.
2. Add the dates, hemp hearts, chia seeds and cashew butter. Whizz until combined.
3. Add the cacao nibs and a pinch of salt, and whizz again.
4. Use your hands to form into balls then serve and enjoy!

Carrot Cake Larabars

Better than the ones you find in the store, these Larabars pack a nutritional punch and taste utterly heavenly.

Serves: 12
Time: 10 mins

- Calories: 105
- Net carbs: 9g
- Protein: 4g
- Fat: 4g

Ingredients:

- 3/4 cup raw almonds
- 1/4 cup raw walnuts
- 3/4 cup pitted dates
- 1/4 cup raisins
- 1/4 cup unsweetened shredded coconut
- 1/4 cup dried pineapple chunks
- 2 tablespoons shredded carrots

Method:

1. Line an 8 x 8" baking tray then pop to one side.
2. Grab your high-speed blender and add the nuts. Whizz until it forms a paste.
3. Add the dates and raisings and whizz until combined.
4. Throw in the remaining ingredients and whizz again.
5. Transfer into the baking tray then press down firmly.
6. Pop into the fridge then cut into 12 bars.
7. Serve and enjoy.

Easy Banana Coconut Cookies

Can you believe that these banana cookies only use two ingredients?? Try them and you'll be amazed at how good they are.

Serves: 5
Time: 30 mins

- Calories: 182
- Net carbs: 12g
- Protein: 2g
- Fat: 15g

Ingredients:

- 1 banana
- 3/4 cup unsweetened shredded coconut

Method:

1. Preheat your oven to 350°F and grease a baking sheet. Pop to one side.
2. Grab your food processor and add the banana and coconut.
3. Whizz until combined.
4. Drop the batter onto the baking sheet then bake in the oven for 25 minutes until golden.
5. Serve and enjoy.

Coconut Almond Butter Truffles

I just can't get enough of these easy bites. A perfect treat after a workout or whenever the fancy takes you, they're ready fast and disappear even faster.

Serves: 5
Time: 20 mins

- Calories: 130
- Net carbs: 4g
- Protein: 2g
- Fat: 12g

Ingredients:

- 1/4 cup coconut butter
- 2 tablespoons almond butter
- 1/4 teaspoon almond extract
- Pinch of salt

For the chocolate dip…

- 1 teaspoon unsweetened cocoa powder
- 1/2 tablespoon coconut oil

Method:

1. Grab a medium bowl and add the coconut and almond butter. Stir well to combine.
2. Add the almond extra and salt and stir again.
3. Pop into the freezer for 10 minutes to firm up slightly.
4. Remove from the freezer then use your hands to roll into balls.
5. Pop back into the freezer for 5 more minutes.
6. Meanwhile, make the chocolate dip by melting the coconut oil in the microwave and stirring in the cocoa powder.
7. Remove the bites from the freezer and dip into the chocolate.
8. Pop back into the freezer and then serve and enjoy.

Super Easy Brownies

It's hard to believe that these brownies are actually 'clean'. The addition of those bananas makes them perfectly light, creamy and delicious.

Serves: 4
Time: 30 mins

- Calories: 474
- Net carbs: 37g
- Protein: 33g
- Fat: 14g

Ingredients:

- 3 ripe bananas
- ½ cup creamy almond butter
- Pinch of salt
- 2 tablespoons 100% cocoa powder

Method:

1. Preheat the oven to 350°F and grease a 7 x 11" pan.
2. Grab a bowl and add the bananas and almond butter. Stir well until smooth.
3. Add the cocoa powder and stir again.
4. Pour the batter into the pan and pop into the oven.
5. Bake for 20 minutes until cooked through.
6. Leave to cool for 10-15 minutes then serve and enjoy.

Bye!!

Thanks for coming with me to the very end of this book. If you weren't already convinced of the benefits of eating a wholefood diet, then it should be absolutely clear by now.

Yes, you can shift weight, glow from within, enjoy tons of energy and overcome a bunch of those niggling health problems.

But it's not just about that.

It's about changing the way you look at food. It's about using it to fuel our bodies with the best food available so that we can thrive. It's about enjoying what we eat, savoring every mouthful, slowing down and taking time to enjoy what we're putting into our bodies and sharing it with others.

It's about being grateful for what we have and allowing ourselves to make the best possible choices for our health.

Because as we know, it's easier not to care. It's easier to just rock up at a takeout and grab whatever food we feel like eating. It seems better to let someone else do all the hard work for us, even if that means making food choices that aren't the best for our bodies.

Starting today, I want that all to change.

Embrace your body and accept it for what it is. Enjoy your food. Make those food choices which nourish you from within, instead of stealing your health and your energy. Keep your taste buds happy, never ever starve yourself and more of all, enjoy this wonderful food we've been given.

BTW...

If you've enjoyed this book, would you mind taking a moment or two to leave a review on Amazon? It would make a massive difference to me and might even help me right a follow up to this book. Thank you.

Made in the USA
Middletown, DE
04 June 2020